Hoecakes, Hambone, and All That Jazz

PROJECT SPONSORS

Missouri Center for the Book
Western Historical Manuscript Collection, University of
    Missouri–Columbia

SPECIAL THANKS

Christine Montgomery, Photographic Specialist, State
    Historical Society of Missouri, Columbia
Amy Arnold, State Historical Society of Missouri, Columbia
Claudia Powell, Graphic Specialist, Western Historical
    Manuscript Collection, University of Missouri–Columbia
Dr. Arvarh Strickland, Professor Emeritus, University of
    Missouri–Columbia
John Viessman, Museum Curator, Missouri Department of
    Natural Resources
Elizabeth Wilson, Inman E. Page Library, Lincoln University

AND THANKS to those friends who shared their personal
photographs with us

    Eliot Battle, Columbia
    Betty Trout Brown, Wright City, Warren County
    Charles Fry, Mexico, Audrain County
    Spencer Galloway
    Doris Handy, Fulton, Callaway County
    Dorothy M. Kitchen, Sedalia, Pettis County
    Irene Marcus, Kansas City
    Margot McMillen
    Leonard Pryor, Kansas City
    Brett Rogers, William Woods University, Fulton

MISSOURI HERITAGE READERS

General Editor, Rebecca B. Schroeder

Each Missouri Heritage Reader explores a particular aspect of the state's rich cultural heritage. Focusing on people, places, historical events, and the details of daily life, these books illustrate the ways in which people from all parts of the world contributed to the development of the state and the region. The books incorporate documentary and oral history, folklore, and informal literature in a way that makes these resources accessible to all Missourians.

Intended primarily for adult new readers, these books will also be invaluable to readers of all ages interested in the cultural and social history of Missouri.

BOOKS IN THE SERIES

Hoecakes, Hambone, and All That Jazz

African American Traditions in Missouri

ROSE M. NOLEN

University of Missouri Press
Columbia and London

Library of Congress Cataloging-in-Publication Data

Nolen, Rose M., 1935–
Hoecakes, hambone, and all that jazz : African American traditions in
Missouri / Rose M. Nolen.
p. cm. — (Missouri heritage readers)
Includes bibliographical references (p.) and index.
ISBN 0-8262-1501-7 (alk. paper)
1. African Americans—Missouri—Social life and customs.
2. African Americans—Missouri—History.
3. Missouri—Social life and customs.
4. Missouri—Race relations.
I. Title. II. Series.
E185.93.M7 N65 2003
305.896'0730778—dc22
2003017588

♾™ This paper meets the requirements of the
American National Standard for Permanence of Paper
for Printed Library Materials, Z39.48, 1984.

Designer: Stephanie Foley
Typesetter: Foley Design
Printer and binder: Thomson-Shore, Inc.
Typefaces: Attic and Times New Roman

To my Missouri family—

particularly to the members
of the seventh generation

CONTENTS

PREFACE

Like all of our United States, Missouri is a land of many cultures.
The customs and traditions of Missourians, their "folkways,"
have come with emigrants from many countries and regions. This
book will focus on the descendants of those pioneers in Missouri
who were emigrants with a difference. They were the descendants of Africans brought to America in chains, aboard slave
ships. They came to Missouri as slaves.

Their ancestors' way of life had been radically different from
that of their captors and their owners, their homeland different
from their new land. Just as their ways were strange to their owners, who were of European ancestry, their owners' ways were
strange to them. Missouri's black pioneers brought with them a
rich and distinct cultural heritage, customs and traditions deeply
rooted in their ancestral past. But because they were captives,
they were forced eventually to take on the cultural practices of
their captors, and the visible surfaces of their own culture began
to slip away.

Nevertheless, by combining memories of traditions handed
down through generations with their life experiences, black people fashioned a new culture. By weaving the threads of the past
through the fabric of the present, they designed an exotic, colorful backdrop with which to drape their landscape. No longer
African, they were now African Americans.

In their new lives as slaves, they created customs and traditions appropriate to their living conditions. As they moved from
slavery toward freedom, they continually reshaped their lives to
adapt to the new situations they faced.

In many ways, the lifestyles of today's African Americans in
Missouri continue to reflect the cultural traditions of their fore-
bears. Just as the creation of the Negro spiritual led to gospel,

ragtime, jazz, and the blues, other customs from the African American past have evolved to become mainstays of today's everyday life.

ACKNOWLEDGMENTS

I am sincerely grateful to all the wonderful people who assisted me in researching and writing this book, including archivists, librarians, researchers, and earlier writers. I owe a special thanks to all those who generously allowed me to use their photographs.

Hoecakes, Hambone,
and All That Jazz

INTRODUCTION

Among the first black residents in what is now Missouri were slaves brought by French explorers in the 1720s to work in the mines of the old Ste. Genevieve District of the Louisiana Territory. (Painting by Oscar Berninghaus, Walker photo, Missouri Resources Division, courtesy State Historical Society of Missouri, Columbia)

A LTHOUGH slavery is a painful subject, it is important to understand how and why certain customs and traditions became part of the lifestyle of an enslaved people. Some African Americans in Missouri are the descendants of slaves brought to the Louisiana Territory by the French or, decades later, by the Spanish. In 1719, an agent of the Company of the Indies, formed to develop the Mississippi Valley for the French, requested slaves to search for the lead and silver he hoped to find in what is now Missouri's eastern Ozarks. A year later Philippe Francois Renault, a French mining engineer, arrived, bringing with him a few additional slaves he had purchased in the West Indies, to develop lead mines in the St. Francois Mountains area, present-day Washington and St. Francois Counties.

Slaves later worked as field hands, domestics, and laborers in the lead and salt mines. They lived under a set of laws known as the *Code Noir,* the "Black Code," which had been issued by France's Louis XIV in 1685 and become law in the Louisiana colony in 1724. Although the French king considered slaves property that could be bought and sold, he set up codes to govern their treatment by their owners. The *Code Noir* required owners to provide food, clothing, and shelter for their slaves. It prevented owners from requiring work on Sundays and holidays. The code made it possible for some slaves to earn money by working for others during their free time.

When the Spanish took control of the Louisiana territory in the 1760s, they did not rescind the French code, but some rules did change. Under the French, slaves could sue their owners if they felt their rights had been violated. Under the Spanish, slaves were still able to sue their owners and could also buy their freedom. Some slaves took advantage of these privileges; in 1773, a slave named Colas sued the estate of Jean Baptiste Labastide, claiming his owner had owed him money for a bed, a table, and a partition wall he had constructed. Some slaves saved the money they earned and purchased their freedom and the freedom of members of their families.

During the French and Spanish colonial period, the Catholic European rulers believed it was their duty to convert the people their representatives conquered. As the explorer Robert de LaSalle said in 1682, when claiming the Louisiana Territory in the name of the king, "his Majesty [Louis XIV] . . . would annex no country to his crown without making it his chief care to establish the Christian religion therein." Louis XIV and the rulers who succeeded him sent missionaries to convert

Native Americans and expected slave owners to instruct their slaves in the Catholic faith and have them baptized. Owners were also required to allow slaves to be officially married, and they were not to separate families by selling individual members. Both women and men could hold property, and a married woman kept title to any property she brought into a marriage.

While the Black Code was supposed to be the law, there were few officials to enforce it in Upper Louisiana, and some slave owners tended to neglect the rules set down in France or Spain. In the colonial period, for example, Ste. Genevieve parish recorded only fourteen slave marriages but nearly five hundred baptisms of slave children.

A small population of free blacks, people who had purchased their own freedom or had been freed by their owners, lived in Upper Louisiana after the founding of Ste. Genevieve, in the 1750s, and Pierre de LaClede's founding of St. Louis in 1764. They were known as freedmen and -women, and in 1791 about sixty-four free blacks lived in and around St. Louis and Ste. Genevieve. Nicolas de Finiels, a French military surveyor visiting French settlements in the Mississippi Valley in the 1790s, wrote that free blacks and mulattoes served as hunters, boatmen, and riverboat skippers, some conducting trade up the rivers. "They are more active and vigorous than the whites; they endure hard labor more courageously. And they could become as good warriors as they are hunters."

Some freed people earned their living by farming, hunting, and working as domestics. Several, women as well as men, became prosperous landowners. Researcher Judith Gilbert examined legal documents relating to Jeannette Fourchet, or Forchet, a free black woman, and wrote of her life and achievements in "Esther and Her Sisters," in the summer 1996 *Gateway Heritage*. Born a slave in the Illinois country east of the Mississippi River, Fourchet was in St. Louis a year after the founding of the settlement; records show she received the grant of a lot from LaClede in 1765. She married Gregerre, a blacksmith, and the couple had four children. Gregerre's death in 1770 was the first recorded in the St. Louis Old Cathedral's register of burials and baptisms. After her husband's death, Fourchet supported her family by operating a home laundry and by farming on land she received from the Spanish government in 1773. Although she was illiterate, she complied with colonial law and tradition and later that year produced an inventory of her property as part of a prenuptial contract for her second marriage: She declared ownership of a house, a small piece of farmland in St. Louis, seven cows, four sows, one dozen hens, and a cock. She married a freedman named Valentin, who was a gunsmith, hunter, and trapper. She was again widowed in 1790, and by then she had acquired another sixty-seven acres of land and household furnishings of substantial value. Historian Christine Williams examined the documents that have survived and concluded that Fourchet was "an intelligent, industrious, and fair-minded woman." According to Williams, however, even Fourchet could not survive the changes occurring at the turn of the nineteenth century as St. Louis became more settled. When she died in 1803, she had little to leave her daughter Susanna except her home. Susanna had worked to pay off the loan against the house, so her mother left it to her in her will, "because it belongs to her by right."

Jacques Clamorgan, a native of the West Indies, came to St. Louis in the 1780s. He was a fur trader, merchant, financier, and land speculator, and he involved himself in many business ventures. He was one of the founders of the Company of the Explorers of the Upper Missouri, which sent expeditions up the Missouri River in search of an all-water route to the Pacific Ocean in the late 1790s, prior to the Lewis and Clark expedition. Historian Lawrence Christensen writes that Clamorgan "could trace his ancestry to Welsh, French, Portuguese, and probably African antecedents," and according to his contemporaries he "lived entirely with women of color."

Esther, the most successful "woman of color" in St. Louis during the 1790s, became Clamorgan's mistress and business confidante. She had been a slave and became Clamorgan's property when her owner defaulted on a debt. Contemporaries described Esther as a beautiful, clever, high-spirited woman, who managed Clamorgan's household, entertained his business associates, and handled his personal affairs when he was away from home. In 1793, when he was starting the exploration company, he tried to protect part of his assets by freeing Esther and putting some of his properties in her name. He gave her the house and lot adjoining his house and used his influence to obtain for her a full city block across the street from the two houses. He also allowed Esther to purchase her daughter, and she began to undertake business on behalf of her family.

When Clamorgan later began choosing younger, mulatto women as companions, Esther, who could not read, became distrustful of him and refused to sign any papers he put before her, fearing that he would cheat her out of her property. Clamorgan became persistent and abusive in his demands, and she left his house in 1797, carrying the deeds to her property with her. Years of lawsuits between them followed, as Clamorgan tried to get the property back, but when he died in 1814, he left his four young children from three different liaisons in Esther's care. Historian Julie Winch writes, "Esther proved a faithful guardian [in] raising Clamorgan's children."

In 1803, when the United States purchased the Louisiana Territory from France, slavery was already well established in Upper Louisiana, with an estimated fifteen hundred slaves in the territory. Most worked at clearing land for farms and planting and harvesting the crops. Some worked in the lead mines, often rented by mine owners from local slaveholders. In 1803, one owner rented a slave to work in the mines for fifteen dollars a month. In the larger settlements, some worked in businesses or as servants in the homes of the wealthy.

During the later years of Spanish rule of the Louisiana Territory, a few Americans had established settlements west of the Mississippi River. In the 1780s Colonel George Morgan of New Jersey developed plans for a large settlement below the mouth of the Ohio River in what is now the Missouri Bootheel. He named it New Madrid, and while he never settled there, others came in response to his promotion of the place and established the first American settlement in Upper Louisiana in 1789. George Lorimier, who had sided with the British during the Revolutionary War, moved west of the Mississippi River in 1787 and took the oath of allegiance to the Spanish king. He established Cape Girardeau in 1793 and began to draw settlers from the East. Moses Austin came to what is now Washington County in 1797, and with the help of slaves, using techniques he had learned in Virginia, he soon revolutionized mining in the area. By 1799 Daniel Boone and several members of his family had settled in the Femme Osage Valley near St. Charles, bringing with them their slaves from Kentucky.

After the Louisiana Purchase, more and more American settlers from the eastern and southern states began to move across the Mississippi River. Many of these new emigrants came from slaveholding states and brought slaves. At first, most slave owners located around settled Mississippi and Missouri River communities like St. Louis, St. Charles, Ste. Genevieve, and Cape Girardeau, but by the time of the War of 1812 with England, some Americans had moved as far west as present-day Cooper, Howard, and Saline Counties.

The attitudes of the new white settlers, and their laws governing slaves, were markedly different from those of the French and Spanish. One of the first actions of the new American government was to set in place a new series of Black Codes similar to those in force in the state of Virginia. Under these codes, established in 1804, slaves could no longer leave their owners' farms without permission, gather in groups without a white official present, or testify against whites in court. Since many of the new settlers were Protestant, rather than Catholic, they were not bound by any particular set of church laws, and the Black Codes adopted by Missouri did not recognize slave marriages or restrict owners from selling slaves' children.

This meant, in most cases, that slave owners no longer kept careful records of births to establish the family identities of slaves. The slave community was left to its own devices in determining relationships. The resulting weakening of the biological family as a unit was probably the most significant loss suffered by slaves during this period of transition from European to American rule.

CHAPTER 1

Early Customs and Traditions

I N 1821, following the Missouri Compromise, Missouri became the twenty-fourth state in the Union. Congress had worked out the compromise to maintain an equal number of slave and free states: Maine joined the Union as a free state, and Missouri was allowed to join as a slave state.

As the new state's population grew, the fertile bottomlands of the Missouri River drew more and more farmers until a line of settlements reached across the state to the border with the Kansas Territory. The larger slave populations came to reside in Missouri River counties such as Callaway, Cole, Boone, Cooper, Howard, Moniteau, Chariton, Lafayette, Ray, Clay, and Jackson. An area in central Missouri had so many settlers from the South that it became known as "Little Dixie." Counties along the Mississippi River in northeast Missouri also drew slaveholders seeking new land, most from Kentucky, Virginia, and Tennessee. By 1840 the slave population of Missouri had grown to more than 57,000. One of the state's largest slave owners was Jabez Smith of Jackson County, who owned as many as 165 slaves at one time.

Most Missouri slaves lived on farms rather than large plantations, usually in crude cabins on the property of their owners. A typical slave cabin was made of roughly sawn logs, daubed with mud, sometimes not much different from the homes of their owners during early settlement. New settlers used slaves to help clear their land, raise crops, and maintain their property. Since workers were scarce in the newly settled areas, landowners found it easier and cheaper to keep slaves than to hire laborers. Owners could also rent slaves out to others to get extra income.

Slaves worked from sunrise to sunset without pay. There were few laws to protect them. Their treatment depended almost entirely on the whims of their owners, who often established rules of behavior based solely on their own best interests. Martha Smith, whose family owned slaves in Pettis County, recorded her memories of how the slave system worked on her family's farm:

> It is melancholy to remember . . . that Uncle Toby, Uncle Jack, and other gray-haired men and women, as well as the younger ones, were compelled to have written permission to leave home, and would come even to me, a little child, when the older members of the family were too busy, to give them a written pass to go to town. The law of the country was to keep the patrol out for the purpose of detecting negroes who might leave home without a pass; and all, the good and the bad, had to obey.

Most Missouri slaves never had the opportunity to learn to read or write, so others wrote much of what we know about them. It appears that owners usually selected names for their slaves, although some few slaves may have kept names of African origin. West-Central Africa used a naming system whereby children were named for the day of the week or the month of the year in which they were born. But these original names changed when spoken in a new language, and their true names were lost.

Africans brought to the United States had been tribal peoples in their native lands, linked in kinship by common ancestors. Under the conditions of slavery, families could be broken at any time. The slave communities soon devised a system of "fictive kinship" that created extended families. When relatives died or were sold, those left behind took over the care of children and others who had been separated from their kinfolk. These caretakers, who were usually older people, often became known as "uncles" and "aunties," and the children taken in became "brothers" and "sisters."

Many people think of slaves brought to the United States as having originally belonged to a particular homogenous group bearing the same physical characteristics and traits and speaking a common language. Although most came from West Africa, the ancestors of the Africans who came to Missouri as slaves were from many kingdoms and many tribes; they ranged in color from very dark to light brown. Some belonged to the taller tribes, such as the Ashanti of the Gold Coast; others to the shorter Bantus from the Congo. Whatever their color, the U.S. census defined anyone with any mixture of African blood as "Negro."

Africa is a continent with many languages and language families. The Republic of Nigeria alone, with a population of about 130 million people, has four major languages used in different parts of the country, as well as dozens of languages (and hundreds of local dialects) used by smaller groups of people. Slave traders, hoping to keep Africans from plotting to organize or escape, would not buy groups who spoke the same language. They also broke up families, forcing those they took as slaves to become accustomed to strangers and learn a new language as best they could.

When modern-day Americans refer to dialects spoken by African Americans as "Black English," many do not realize how this language came into existence. Because slaves did not have common languages, they were forced to speak the language of the field bosses or members of households where they were servants. They received very little instruction, so they learned to use a kind of pidgin English. Sometimes they would use words from their native languages, like "cooter" for turtle, "goobers" for peanuts, and "buckra" for a white man. Some of their words, like "okra" and "gumbo," passed into English and are commonly used today.

As they learned more and more, the slaves spoke a kind of English that was more complex, but it was still not exactly like their owners' language. Because African languages have few consonants at the end of their words, the slaves had trouble saying words like "cold." Since the slaves and servants lived in highly segregated environments, they learned from one another and began to speak alike, passing their own kind of English and their pronunciations on to later generations. Many speakers of "Black English" are simply continuing to use the language of their community, just as whites in Appalachia and along the coast of Maine continue their own ways of talking.

In Missouri, French continued to be spoken in communities such as St. Louis and Ste. Genevieve for several decades after the Louisiana Purchase, and new German immigrants established settlements in which they maintained their native language in church services and business establishments for more than a century. During the years of slavery and afterward, African Americans often learned enough of these languages and the various dialects to communicate in such places as St. Charles, New Melle, Hermann, Bethel, and Concordia.

Instead of common ancestors and common languages, which families had shared in Africa, the enslaved in the United States came to be bound together by skin color, hair texture, and condition of bondage. From this experience a strong sense of community was born. As enslaved people, their survival often depended upon the actions of individuals in the community. If one slave broke the rules, it could, and often did, bring hardship on the group as a whole.

The conditions of their enslavement meant that many slaves knew nothing but slavery. Some heard that they could be free in territories or states bordering Missouri and longed to escape. In spite of the danger to themselves and their community, some tried to escape. The *Marshall Democrat* reported that in Saline County, between 1858 and 1859, twelve

$100 REWARD:

R AN AWAY from the subscriber, living in Boone county, Mo. on Friday the 13th June,

THREE NEGROES,

VIZ DAVE, and JUDY his wife; and JOHN, their son. Dave is about 32 years of age, light color for a full blooded negro— is a good boot and shoe maker by trade : is also a good farm hand. He is about 5 feet 10 or 11 inches high, stout made, and quite an artful, sensible fellow. Had on when he went away, coat and pantaloons of brown woollen jeans, shirt of home made flax linen, and a pair of welted shoes. Judy is rather slender made, about 28 years old, has a very light complexion for a negro; had on a dress made of flax linen, striped with copperas and blue; is a first rate house servant and seam-stress, and a good spinner, and is very full of affectation when spoken to. John is 9 years old, very likely and well grown; is remark-ably light colored for a negro, and is cross-eyed. Had on a pair of brown jeans panta-loons, bleached flax linen shirt, and red flan-nel one under it, and a new straw hat.

I will give the above reward and all reas-onable expenses, if secured any where out of the State, so that I can get them again, or $50 if taken within the State—$30 for Dave alone, and $20 for Judy and John, and the same in proportion out of the state. The a-bove mentioned clothing was all they took with them from home, but it is supposed he had $30 or $40 in cash with him, so that he may buy and exchange their clothing.

WILLIAM LIENTZ.

Boone county, Mo. June 17, 1834:   52-8

Many slaves tried to escape; sometimes whole families ran away together. After the United States bought the Louisiana Territory, the French *Code Noir,* which forbade the separation of families, was no longer in effect, and family members could be sold separately. Considering their slaves valuable property, owners offered rewards for their capture. (State Historical Society of Missouri, Columbia) slaves ran away. Reports of runaways and occasional stories of slaves killing their owners in escape attempts led slave-holders to watch their slaves closely. When a slave ran, the owner was likely to punish the whole slave community until the runaway was caught.

To slave owners their slaves were tied together by color and condition of servitude. The enslaved, on the other hand, chose to bond on the basis of real and "fictive" kinships. Those relationships formed the foundation of community for them and made it possible to endure lives of unremitting labor.

The daily work of enslaved men, women, and children in Missouri varied with their owners and the seasons. On farms, much of the work involved planting in the spring and harvesting the crops in the fall. The main crops produced by Missouri farmers were hemp, tobacco, wheat, corn, oats, hay, and, in the southern part of the state, cotton. In addition many slave owners planted orchards and gardens. They bred livestock, and most farms had cattle, sheep, horses, pigs, and chickens.

In the modern world of tractors, milking machines, and other conveniences, it is hard to imagine the effort required for pioneer families to survive. On small farms with only a few slaves, work was unending. Missouri had some large slave-holders, such as Jabez Smith and John Ragland, the largest slaveholder in Cooper County, who had seventy slaves in 1850. But in *Missouri's Black Heritage,* historians Lorenzo Greene, Gary Kremer, and Antonio Holland report that only 36 of Missouri's 114 counties had "one thousand or more" slaves, and anyone who owned ten slaves was considered rich. Many times owners and slaves worked together, a situation not always welcomed by the enslaved. Slave women often had to work in the fields along with the men. Otherwise women and children helped the owners' wives with the household chores.

They would help plant, tend, and pick the family's fruit and vegetables and preserve them for later use; help cook the three daily meals; prepare the wool and flax to be spun into thread on the spinning wheel; clean the house and take care of the children. Since there were no electric lights, slave women had to fill lanterns and lamps with oil and make candles from tallow or beeswax. Before they could cook, they had to build a fire in the fireplace or the stove. They had to churn cream into butter by hand in large wooden buckets.

With no washing machines or permanent-press fabrics, women had to wash and iron by hand, first drawing the water for the wash from a well or carrying it from a creek, heating it on the stove or over a fire, and filling large washtubs. They put the clothes and household linens into heavy iron pots over fires, either outdoors or in washsheds. After soaking the wash in boiling water with soap they had made, the women scrubbed the clothing or laid it out on a board and beat it with a club before rinsing it. Since there were few clotheslines, they often spread laundry over bushes and fences to dry. Then they had to iron the clothes. As the name suggests, irons were made of heavy cast iron. The woman doing the ironing heated four or five "flatirons" on the cookstove while she worked. It was hot, hard work, and if the owner's wife had a bad temper, she might punish a slave who allowed an iron to get too hot and scorch the clothes.

For those who labored in the fields, tending the crops from which their owners earned a living, work was even harder. Hemp was one of the main crops grown in Missouri. This plant was made into rope and into the twine used to bind bales of cotton. Harvesting hemp was demanding work. Slaves had to cut the tall plants, which grew up to eight feet, and spread them on the ground to dry. Since only the stalks were used, the rest of the plants had to rot away. Workers might either leave plants on the ground to rot from the dew and rain or dunk them in heated water to hurry the process. Once the stalks were ready, workers had to bundle them. On many farms, each slave had to break at least one hundred pounds of hemp

Some large farms had overseers to ensure that everyone—men, women, and children—kept working. (State Historical Society of Missouri, Columbia)

a day. In *Agriculture and Slavery in Little Dixie,* Douglas Hurt quotes a saying of the time: "Small hands . . . can raise and take care of tobacco; hemp requires the stoutest men."

But tobacco, as Hurt writes, still required "many hands to plant, cultivate, tend, harvest and process the crop." It was year-round labor, from preparing the land in January to sowing the tobacco bed, setting the plants, hoeing weeds, then cutting, curing, and shipping the tobacco just in time to start preparing the land for another crop. There were no chemical pesticides. "Slaves picked off the terminal bud and hornworms by hand," Hurt reports.

In addition to planting, harvesting, shucking, or threshing other crops, the slave men also had to construct and repair fences and buildings as well as keep the tools in good repair. They cared for the farm animals and helped butcher those that had been raised for food. Most landowners raised their own cows, and the slaves had to do the daily milking, carry the milk to the house, and process it for the owner's family to use for drinking and cooking.

The children of slaves learned to work from an early age. They did small household tasks such as sweeping or beating the rugs. In wealthy families male slave children sometimes served as footmen. They opened carriage doors for the owners and held the horses until the driver was ready. Girls helped with cooking and serving the meals and cleaning the kitchen.

Enslaved people had no retirement plan. As women got too old for heavy work, they did such jobs as sewing, nursing the sick, serving as midwives, and looking after infants while their mothers worked. Older men sometimes served as herbal doctors or worked repairing farm tools. Since by law slaves were personal property, owners could punish or sell those who were poor workers. Older slaves had to continue working as long as they could.

Since slaves had to devote most of their time to work, it is only natural that one of the African American community's most celebrated traditions grew out of the work experience. At work slaves created the Negro spiritual and the many kindred songs that are the basis for the African American musical tradition. Most of their work was drudgery. Making music was one of the few freedoms they could enjoy, and they used their songs to turn misery and sorrow into art.

Work songs, shout songs, sorrow songs, and jubilees are among the names African Americans gave to these oral compositions. In the tradition of their African ancestors, the slaves would make up the story they wanted to tell, putting into words whatever thoughts came to mind, and pass it along in song. In the African tradition, all events, large and small, work or play, happy or sad, became the stuff of stories that could be put to song. Owners often forbade slaves to talk as they worked, so singing became a way of passing information as well as providing emotional relief and furnishing entertainment. For the slaves, the field shouts or hollers and other

This drawing of a young slave being sold despite his mother's pleas appeared in an English translation of *Wild Sports in the Far West,* an account of the travels of German writer Friederich Gerstaecker, who walked from St. Louis through Arkansas to Louisiana in 1838. He wrote that at slave auctions he had witnessed "some heart-breaking scenes." (State Historical Society of Missouri, Columbia)

forms of the songs that developed were means of communicating with one another. Through this means of communication many slaves learned of freedom. Yet their singing may also have been the reason many slave owners considered the slaves happy and carefree.

The songs would usually begin with one worker singing out a sentence, to which the others would respond by singing back. In this way, the form of leader and chorus, call and response, an African American musical tradition began. The songs that the slaves used while they worked soon found a new home in what has come to be called the "invisible church."

Although they were not required to do so, most owners introduced their slaves to Christian teachings, often by reading to them from the Bible. Some demanded attendance at their churches, of whatever denomination, where slaves sat in a balcony or in a separate area in the back of the church. Just as French and Spanish slaveholders had converted many slaves to Catholicism, the slaveholders emigrating from the Upper South introduced their particular Protestant beliefs to those they owned. Most owners considered the slaves simple people, likely to accept the call to religion and, they hoped, obey their owners while they were on earth in the expectation of rewards in heaven. It was clearly in the best interests of the slaveholders to teach the enslaved the evils of stealing, lying, and disobeying, and so most instructed slaves on the Christian virtues.

Owners probably felt that they had made good slaves of their people when they heard songs from the nearby slave cabins:

> I've got a robe,
> You've got a robe,
> All of God's children got a robe.
> When I get to heaven goin' to put on my robe,
> Goin' to shout all over God's heav'n.

Some slaves, however, persisted in hoping that they could gain their freedom on earth, either by buying themselves from their owners or by escaping to the North. Furthermore, although owners tried to teach slaves that it was the owners' right to hold them in bondage, most slaves found it hard to understand why some men should be masters and some slaves.

Perhaps, it was those of this mind who sang out:

> Hear that freedom train a-coming, coming, coming,
> Hear that freedom train a-coming, coming, coming,
> Hear that freedom train a-coming, coming, coming,
> Get on board, oh, oh, get on board.

Some of the enslaved found that for all the preaching about goodness and kindness they heard, their owners thought nothing of lashing them with a whip or selling them away from their families. Still, most slaves took to heart the words of the Bible, if not their owners' interpretations of those words, and embraced Christianity wholeheartedly. Many came to feel that they had found a friend in Jesus and that He wanted them to be free, even if their owners did not. And for the slave, freedom was everything. And so they sang:

> Oh, freedom! Oh, freedom! . . .
> An' befo' I'd be a slave, I'll be buried in my grave
> An' go home to my Lord an' be free.

After attending the owners' churches on Sunday, slaves might have time for themselves. Then they held their own church meetings in one of their cabins or in secret places in the fields in the evening. There they chose one of their own as preacher, worshiped in their own spirited style, and re-created their work songs to include spiritual messages. These secret meetings came to be known as the "invisible church."

Some owners allowed their slaves to hold "camp meetings" under their watchful eye. These early revivals, while supposedly spiritual in nature, also became social and recreational occasions for owners as well as slaves. In some cases, owners sold whiskey to those not inclined to spend the day in worship. Reports of witnesses indicate that some slave owners used camp meetings to encourage their slaves to get drunk and hold wrestling contests for the amusement of owners and their guests. These stories aside, most blacks, slave and free, were serious in their beliefs, expressed in their intensely spiritual style of religious worship, which, along with the Negro spiritual, took root in the slave experience, and continues in many African American churches today.

Many other traditional practices grew out of the conditions of slavery on rural Missouri farms. The daily diet of the slaves depended largely on the generosity or the meanness of their owners. Some slaves reported being barely fed, having to rely on beans, potatoes, and cornbread for their meals. Others were able to have their own vegetable gardens, which provided such produce as greens and yams. Still, cornmeal, molasses, and pork leavings were often staples of the slave diet.

According to some slave narratives, food allowances were far from generous. One former slave, Eliza Overton, who lived in Ste. Genevieve County, said that her family often ran out of the food they got as an allowance, and so her mother would sometimes hit one of her owner's hogs over the head, hide it under the cabin, and butcher it at night.

For most slaves, making the meager ingredients that were available into tasty meals took a lot of imagination. The custom of taking "a little bit of this" and adding "a little bit of that" resulted in the first recipes for soul food. The slaves, familiar with the one-pot cooking style that was a part of their African heritage, did what they could with the leftovers they received from the owners' tables, sometimes flavoring their food with a rabbit or possum they had managed to catch.

This photo of "Aunt Kitty" appeared in a booklet relating to General David Thomson, founder of Georgetown in Pettis County. Thomson owned more than sixty slaves. The photograph of Aunt Kitty was made by Latour's Photographic Gallery and Studio in Sedalia. (Collection of Rose Nolen)

When there was not much food, the adult slaves might eat most of the ingredients in the pot to fill their stomachs. The children then had to rely on the juice, or "pot likker," at the bottom of the pot for their nourishment.

To satisfy their hunger, slaves had to rely on their own skills. Preparing a hoecake, which would today be called a corncake, required care and coordination: First the cook had to make a fire out of whatever twigs and brush he or she could gather. Mixing a little meal, water, and salt together on the greased blade of a hoe until the batter was thick enough to fry, the cook slanted the hoe carefully into the fire, letting the cake bake until the top bubbled. Finally, the cake had to be flipped so that it turned over and fell back onto the blade of the hoe, where it could be baked until brown. A slave who failed to master the flip could easily lose his or her day's meal.

The personal cleanliness and grooming of slaves was not something owners usually thought about. They might pass their old clothing along to the slaves as hand-me-downs; otherwise, slave women sewed for themselves and their families. A typical wardrobe consisted of dresses for the women, brown pants and cotton shirts for the men, and long shirts or gowns for boys and girls. Although winter coats were sometimes available, shoes often were not, and some slaves went barefoot summer and winter.

The care of their hair was particularly troublesome to slaves. The combs used by their owners, which they sometimes received as gifts, were unsuitable for the texture of their hair and hurt their scalps. Their African ancestors had carved combs from wood. In the New World, slaves had no personal possessions and had to use whatever was given them or do without. Because they could not care for it properly, hair became a source of constant agony to many slaves. Uncombed, it matted to the scalp, and problems such as ringworm developed. They often had to use feedbags, which might be infested with parasites, for bedding, and their scalps sometimes became infected and developed painful sores.

Slaves who worked as domestics sometimes tried to duplicate the grooming habits of their owners to keep up an appearance that would not be offensive to them. As author Willie Morrow notes in *Four Hundred Years without a Comb,* "The women house slaves who prepared and served the master's food had to keep their hair covered, not only to keep hair from falling into the food, but also hide its lack of grooming." After being washed, their hair smelled sour when it dried, because of its tendency to mat to their heads. If shears were available, some slaves used them to cut off their hair. Most males, however, avoided this practice because the heat of the sun was painful on their shorn heads during long hours in the fields. Often, the slaves would use lard, chicken fat, mutton tallow, or butter to condition their skin and groom their hair. This only made matters worse when the oils attracted flies and other insects, so the custom began of keeping the head covered with a cap or rag.

The coverings served three purposes: They shielded the hair from the owners' view; they protected the scalp from the heat of the sun; and they kept flies and insects away. Today some African Americans still feel more comfortable with hats, caps, or cloths covering their hair.

Missouri slaves sometimes had Saturday afternoons to do their own work. Some used the time to make small items that they could sell for money of their own. Many slaves were skilled artisans and could fashion ax handles or horse whips, do fancy needlework, and produce other special goods to sell. The slaves also drew upon African tradition to create entertainment for themselves and others during their free time on Saturday evenings, beginning the custom of Saturday night celebrations. They might use the occasion to "make Juba," a dance characterized by lively rhythm and clapping of hands.

Ole Rabbit, from *Old Rabbit the Voodoo and Other Sorcerers,* by Mary Alicia Owen, contemplates his next adventure. The author's sister, Juliette A. Owen, drew most of the illustrations for the book. (State Historical Society of Missouri, Columbia)

The "jogs and shuffles," animated dances from their home-land, had been passed down to them, and they, in turn, passed them down to their children and grandchildren. Or they might make up new songs. Occasionally, there would be a fiddler or a banjo player who had built an instrument and was willing to play. A boy who grew up in Bethel Colony in Shelby County, a German settlement, remembered that slaves of a nearby landowner would come to get banjo strings from his music-teacher father. When he would take no pay from them, the slaves brought the family baskets of nuts and apples in exchange.

Storytelling was another favorite amusement. This honored oral tradition served to lighten the burden of lives spent in endless work. Like their music, the slaves' stories were often created out of their experiences. They found special delight in stories about the tricks played on cruel masters by their slaves and the slyness and cunning the tricksters used to outwit their owners.

They took the raw stuff of their work lives, relationships, triumphs, and tragedies and drew on their knowledge of native animals to enrich their repertoires. The fox's cunning, the turtle's slow pace, and the rabbit's quickness were often used to add flair to their adventures.

Mary Alicia Owen of St. Joseph took down many of the folk narratives she heard as she was growing up and published her collection, *Old Rabbit the Voodoo and Other Sorcerers,* in London in the 1890s. She had collected a rich variety of tales about Old Rabbit, Old Woodpecker, Old Blue Jay, the Bee King, and other creatures of the forest.

CHAPTER 2

Dreams of Freedom

T HE African American tradition of protest was born in slavery. While the slaves had limited means to free themselves from bondage, the Negro spiritual expresses their yearning for freedom. The desire to escape the terrible conditions of slavery burned in many souls. While most of those born into slavery remained enslaved until death or Emancipation freed them, some used every means at their disposal to put distance between themselves and their owners.

The fact that there were no major slave uprisings in Missouri did not mean that the slaves were happy with their lot, as many of their owners wanted to believe. Slaves protested their condition in a variety of ways. Some resorted to desperate measures such as self-mutilation, for example, cutting off their fingers in the hope that this would prevent their being sold away from their families. Others resisted by destroying their oppressor's property. A few even went so far as to try to murder their owners or members of the owner's family. But researchers have found that in Missouri most protest was nonviolent: work slowdowns, pretended illness, breaking of tools, or destruction of property.

Escape was the most popular form of protest. And probably the most famous escape from Missouri was that of William Wells Brown, who became the first black man born in America to write plays, a novel, and accounts of his travels in Europe, as well as a "slave narrative." He also wrote the first study by an African American from the South about life in its slave communities.

Brown, whose mother, Elizabeth, was a slave and whose father was his owner's half-brother, was born near Lexington, Kentucky, in 1815. Their owner brought the youngster and his mother to Missouri in 1827 to live on a farm north of St. Louis near the Mississippi River. When William was thirteen, his owner moved closer to St. Louis and rented him out to work. During his teenage years, he constantly tried to escape the cruelties of slavery, but each time he ran away, he was captured and severely punished.

His brothers and sisters had been sold away, and when his mother was sold to a St. Louis man, Brown persuaded her to flee with him to Canada. They made their attempt in 1833. Slave hunters captured them after eleven days. Brown's mother was sold immediately, and he never saw her again. Brown was later sold to a St. Louis steamboat owner. The next year he accompanied the family on a trip to Ohio. When the boat stopped in Cincinnati, he simply walked off and never returned, following "my friend, truly the slaves' friend, the North Star."

In 1847, two years after the Boston Anti-Slavery office published *Narrative of the Life of Frederick Douglass, an American Slave,* it published the *Narrative of William W. Brown, a Fugitive Slave.* In 1853, in London, Brown published *Clotel, or the President's Daughter,* and, in 1858, his play, "The Escape; or, a Leap for Freedom." He traveled extensively in Europe and lectured in Europe and the United States. A. G. Brown and Company of Boston published Brown's *My Southern Home: or, The South and Its People* in 1880, four years before his death.

Another well-publicized escape by a Missouri slave was that of John Anderson, who first belonged to Moses Burton, a tobacco farmer in Howard County. According to Patrick Brode, who wrote *The Odyssey of John Anderson,* Anderson's father was "almost white," a steward on a Missouri river steamer, who escaped shortly after his son's birth. Anderson later remembered his mother as "a great big spirit, something like me, and wouldn't stand being beat about and knocked around." After a confrontation with the owner's wife, John's mother was sold away when he was seven. Mrs. Burton took care of the young slave, who was then called Jack. He grew up in the Burton family, and when he was old enough, his owners put him in charge of a tobacco crop and made him a supervisor of the other slaves on the farm.

In the 1850s, John fell in love with Maria Tomlin, the enslaved daughter of a free black man in Fayette, the widowed mother of two children. John and Maria married by slave custom, and Anderson planned to earn enough money to purchase his family's freedom. But his relationship with his owner became increasingly hostile when his secret visits to Maria made him late for work, and Burton sold him to a man in Saline County.

After spending a brief time at the new farm, Anderson took a mule and ran away. On the third day of his escape, he encountered a Fayette farmer, Seneca Digges, who suspected he was a runaway. When Anderson ran, Digges ordered the four slaves with him to capture him. In trying to escape his pursuers, Anderson suddenly found himself face to face with Digges, and in a struggle, he stabbed the farmer and escaped. He finally made his way to Canada in November 1853, a year in which over one thousand runaway slaves crossed the Canadian border. Seneca Digges died from his injuries, and Missouri officials never gave up the effort to have the former slave returned for trial. Anderson changed his name several times, lived quietly, and managed to avoid notice until 1860, when he was identified and arrested.

Brode describes the long trial, which officials in the United States followed closely. Anderson later commented that he "never knew there was so much law in the world as he . . . found in Canada," but he finally won his freedom on a technicality, and in 1861 he went to England, where he gave several lectures and attended a school. The English then decided that he should go to Liberia. Anderson's response was that he had once felt great prejudice against Liberia, "against even the very name of it," but his sponsors persuaded him that he would find his future there. He boarded a ship in December 1862, but biographer Patrick Brode finds no evidence that he ever lived in Liberia and writes that John Anderson's "final destiny became a mystery."

Like Anderson, some slaves tried to reach freedom on their own, but the Underground Railroad aided other Missouri runaways, though not always successfully. It was a network of locations, each situated a day's journey from the next; a guide, called a conductor, would take runaway slaves along the route. They would travel by night, and by day would hide in a barn, cave, or other secret place where they could eat, rest, and sometimes don disguises; then a conductor would lead them on to the next location. The slaves continued until they reached freedom. Following his escape, William Wells Brown became a conductor in Cleveland, Ohio. In 1842, over six months, he led sixty-nine fugitives by boat to Canada. It was a dangerous venture for both those trying to escape and those trying to help them. After the Fugitive Slave Act passed in 1850, federal fugitive slave commissioners could capture and return runaways to their owners in slave states. Slave hunters, eager to collect rewards, often did not take the time to see that their captives received the due process the law required.

Joplin, Potosi, Kansas City, Bethany, and other Missouri cities reportedly had depots on the Underground Railroad, but the National Park Service Underground Railroad Network to Freedom Program has thus far recognized only one such site in Missouri. In 1855, a party hoping to escape crossed the Mississippi on St. Louis's north riverfront "sometime between dusk on May 20 and dawn" the following day, according to Kris Zapalac of the State Historic Preservation Office. When they reached the Illinois shore, slave owners and police were

The Mary Meachum Freedom Crossing on the Mississippi River. (Missouri Department of Natural Resources, State Historic Preservation Office, photo by Kris Zapalac)

waiting to arrest them. Mary Meachum, widow of minister and educator John Berry Meachum, whose St. Louis home was said to have served as the depot, was arrested and charged with having "enticed slaves out of the state." Meachum's home is gone, but the Freedom Crossing site was approved by the National Park Service in autumn 2001.

Sometimes abolitionists in Illinois or the Kansas Territory encouraged slaves to escape. In 1841, three men from Quincy, Illinois, were convicted of attempting to "steal" slaves they were trying to help escape and sentenced to twelve years in the Missouri State Penitentiary. In the winter of 1858, abolitionist John Brown gathered up about a dozen slaves in western Missouri and took them to Chicago; the famous detective Allan Pinkerton saw that they reached Canada.

Rather than trying to escape, some slaves took their owners to court in the hope of gaining their freedom. As early as 1806 the family of Marie Jean Scypion, the daughter of an Indian woman and a black slave, filed suit, claiming that they were free by reason of their Indian ancestry. Marie Jean was born near Fort Chartres, Illinois, the slave of a French priest. The priest gave the young woman to his cousin Madame Boisset as a gift. When Boisset's daughter married, she inherited Marie Jean and took her to St. Louis when she and her husband moved there.

Although Scypion had died in 1802, her family battled through the courts for their freedom for thirty years. In 1838, the U.S. Supreme Court sustained a lower court ruling that freed Scypion's descendants. Documents recently made public by the Missouri State Archives from the St. Louis Circuit Court's records offer dramatic evidence of the extent of slaves' efforts to gain their freedom. According to a recent report, some 280 legal documents filed between 1814 and 1860 include "original handwritten documents in which black men, women, and children petitioned for freedom."

The Dred Scott case became the most famous of the suits in which a slave petitioned the court for his freedom. Scott was born a slave in Virginia, the property of Peter Blow, who settled in St. Louis around 1830. Blow sold Scott to John Emerson, an army surgeon, who took him to live in Illinois and then Wisconsin Territory, both free, during his tours of army duty there. In Wisconsin, Scott met and married Harriet, whose owner transferred her ownership to Emerson. After their return to Missouri, Scott sued for his freedom and the freedom of his wife, on the grounds that by having lived in a free territory, they had become free persons.

The first two trials were held in St. Louis. The first was dismissed on a technicality, but in the second, the Scotts gained

Dred Scott. (Library of Congress)

Harriet Scott. (Library of Congress)

their freedom. The Missouri Supreme Court overturned the decision on appeal, a ruling later upheld by the Federal District Court. The case was argued twice before the U.S. Supreme Court, and in 1857 that court ruled that since Scott, as a slave, was not considered a citizen of the United States, he had no right to sue for his freedom.

Following the famous trial, the Scotts were transferred back to the Blow family, who had supported their suit and subsequently freed them. It was not until Congress passed the Fourteenth Amendment on July 28, 1868, that "all persons born or naturalized in the United States," including African Americans, became citizens of the United States and the state in which they resided.

Still, some Missourians born into slavery gained international fame. One was Father Augustine Tolton, a former slave who became the first nationally recognized black priest in the United States. The French reign, which brought many Catholic missionaries to the Louisiana Territory, ended in the 1760s, but Catholic influence endured through the Spanish reign and far beyond. Some of the American settlers moving into Missouri were Catholic and saw that their slaves became Catholics. Among these were several families from Kentucky who moved into northeast Missouri in the 1840s.

Augustine Tolton, who was to become the first nationally known African American priest, was born on April 1, 1854, to Martha Jane and Peter Paul Tolton, both slaves in Ralls County. Stephen and Susan Elliott owned Martha Jane, who had been a wedding present to Susan Elliott and had come to Missouri from Kentucky with the newlyweds, leaving behind family and friends she would never see again. Peter Paul Tolton belonged to a neighboring Catholic family, the James Hagers. Peter Paul and Martha Jane had married in a Catholic ceremony in St. Peter's Church at Brush Creek. They lived together on the Elliott farm, but Peter Paul continued to work for the Hagers. The children of the marriage were to belong to the Elliotts.

Father Augustine Tolton was born a slave in Ralls County. He escaped with his mother, brother, and sister when he was seven years old. He wrote that a reward of two hundred dollars was offered for their capture. (Tolton Collection, University Archives, Brenner Library, Quincy University)

Young Augustine was the second of three children born to
Martha Jane and baptized in the church in Brush Creek. When
the Civil War began, Peter Paul Tolton escaped and went to St.
Louis to join the Union army. He died from dysentery a short
time later, but Martha Jane did not know of his death until
the war ended. She decided to try to get to the free state of
Illinois with her three children. They walked to Hannibal,
where Union soldiers helped them find a boat to cross the Mississippi River. According to a letter from a Union officer in
Hannibal, an Underground Railroad station in the town was
helping many slaves cross into Illinois, but Tolton recalled
that his family crossed alone, with his mother rowing the boat.

She found lodging in the black community in Quincy,
Illinois, and she and Augustine got jobs in a cigar factory. The
family attended St. Boniface Church, and Martha Jane tried
to help her son get an education. He enrolled in the parochial
school but was forced to withdraw because of objections by
some white parents. He later attended what was called Colored
School Number One in a small log cabin, but he was much
older than the other students, and when the Toltons started
attending St. Lawrence Church, its Irish priest, Father Peter
McGirr, insisted that Augustine attend St. Lawrence School.
Augustine learned the Latin Mass, and, according to biographers, began to serve mass daily before going to work. Father
McGirr talked to him about becoming a priest, and priests at
St. Francis College, impressed with Augustine's dedication
and willingness to help others, began to tutor him. He later
registered as a student at St. Francis, now Quincy University,
and helped the Franciscans, who had begun a parish for people of color in Quincy, get the new parish established.

Friends in the church continued to encourage Augustine to
study for the priesthood and tried to help him enroll in a seminary. Because of his race no seminary in the United States
would accept him, but with the assistance of friends he applied
to the Propaganda College in Rome. He was accepted, stud-

ied there for six years, and was ordained in Rome in 1886.

Father Gus (as he was known) had hoped to go to Africa as a missionary, but his superiors in Rome decided he should return home. He became pastor of St. Joseph's, the church for African Americans in Quincy. His eloquence brought both black and white Catholics to St. Joseph's, but his popularity also inspired hostility among some black Protestant pastors and some white Catholic priests. He found that hard to bear and asked to be transferred to Chicago. In Chicago, Father Tolton founded St. Monica's Church, named for the mother of St. Augustine, where he worked until his death. He was forty-three years old when he died from heat stroke in Chicago in 1897.

Another former slave gained fame through his love of horses. In Missouri, when the subject is horses, one man's name generally comes to mind: Tom Bass, born in 1859 of a slave mother on the farm of Eli Bass in Boone County. The famous "Bass bit," which for many years has been considered standard equipment in stables throughout the country, was his brainchild. He never patented his invention or earned money from it, but his role as inventor has never been disputed.

Bass's grandparents, Presley and Eliza Gray, raised him. When the Civil War ended, Presley Gray became one of the founders of Log Providence Baptist Church in the Three Creek settlement in Boone County. Gray and his sons are credited with being among those who helped clear the ground and construct the original log church. When the Grays moved to Columbia shortly after the war, their young grandson had already acquired an interest in horses. He chose to remain on the Bass farm, where he tended and trained horses. From the weekend livestock sales, which he attended, he learned about the business of horse trading.

At one of these events he met Joseph Potts, a prominent horseman from Mexico, Missouri. Through Potts, Bass obtained a job with a hotel owner in Mexico as a bellboy and carriage driver. He soon earned a reputation as a skilled trainer,

Tom Bass on Belle Beach. With patience, skill, and love, Bass taught Belle Beach, "the greatest show mare in American history," to dance to "The Blue Danube" and "Turkey in the Straw" and to trot backward. (State Historical Society of Missouri, Columbia)

and Potts hired him at his Mexico Horse Sales Company. While working there, he invented the bit that was less painful for horses and made it possible to train and show the animals without abusing them.

In 1883, Bass opened his own stables on four acres of land he purchased north of Mexico. He also opened another stable in Kansas City, where he kept livery horses and taught horseback riding and horse training. Organizers of the 1893 Columbian Exposition in Chicago invited Bass to compete in the horse show at the Exposition, where the "Champion of the World" would be crowned. He decided to take a five-year-old, Miss Rex, and the judges picked Miss Rex as World Champion.

Tom Bass was recognized as a leading horseman whose clientele included many rich and famous horse lovers, such as St. Louis brewers August and Adolph Busch, and the Swift and Armour families, who had made a fortune in meatpacking. He earned many awards, trophies, and medals for his work, but he could not escape the sting of discrimination. Like other men of his race, he was denied many privileges. Still, his accomplishments were great and many. On the occasion of her Diamond Jubilee in 1897, Queen Victoria of England invited him to give a command performance, and three presidents visited his stables in Mexico: William McKinley, Theodore Roosevelt, and William Taft. Bass was another son of a Missouri slave who became a giant in his field. His name is still remembered in Missouri and known in horse circles throughout the nation.

The few free black men and women throughout the state fared little better in the matter of personal freedom under Missouri law than those who were held in slavery. According to *Missouri's Black Heritage,* a series of repressive laws severely limited the "freedom" of free blacks. The state legislature passed laws to prevent free blacks from traveling or gathering in groups. They could not possess weapons. An 1835 law forced each person to purchase a license, costing from five hundred to one thousand dollars, to reside in any Missouri county. To get such a license, a person had to either post a bond or get a white person to act as his or her security. Though free, a black could not serve as a witness in court. Another law required all county courts to bind "all free Negroes and mulattos between the ages of seven and twenty one as apprentices or servants." An 1847 law made it illegal to teach blacks, slave or free, to read or write. Slave owners considered free blacks a threat.

In 1839 groups in several communities in the state formed the Missouri Colonization Society, an affiliate of the American Colonization Society, and sought to organize the transportation of free blacks back to Africa. As early as 1776,

Thomas Jefferson had proposed a plan for the colonization in Africa of free blacks living in Virginia. The American Colonization Society, founded in 1816, first sent those who were willing to immigrate to Sierra Leone; in 1821 the society purchased a permanent location near Monrovia, named for President James Monroe, for a colony of African Americans. In 1847, the new colony, Liberia, declared its independence, and Monrovia became its capital.

The colonization plan appealed to only a few former slaves. Most of the freed blacks now had families scattered throughout the United States. In the first fifteen years of the Colonization Society's existence, only eighty-three blacks from Missouri had gone to Africa. In 1855 the state legislature made sixty dollars available to the society for each person who agreed to be transported, but this made little difference. The involuntary emigrants from Africa had invested their free labor in the new country, and many felt that they were now Missourians, not Africans, even though in Missouri, as in many slave states, life was not easy for freedmen and women.

Many of the free blacks in Missouri had bought their freedom and that of their families. W. P. Brooks of St. Louis purchased his freedom after moving to Missouri from Virginia in 1842. According to *Missouri's Black Heritage,* Brooks operated a wood and coal business for about ten years. He became active with the Underground Railroad and worked to provide education for blacks. In 1857 John Lane of St. Louis purchased his freedom for twelve hundred dollars and went on to become a property owner and businessman. Since freedmen and women often had been slaves and continued to have to bear many of the same hardships as slaves, many remained closely tied to the slave community. Freed people often used their limited resources to assist the slaves in any way they could. Some bought slaves and let them work out their freedom.

One man who did this was Hiram Young of Independence, who owned a wagon factory and a large farm in the 1850s and was often seen buying slaves at auctions. Young, however, trained his slaves and allowed them to work out the price of their freedom. He knew what it was like to be a slave. Born of a slave mother in Tennessee, he had exhibited a talent for whittling as he grew up. His owner rewarded his talent by paying for the rake, hoe, and axe handles he whittled for use by the plantation slaves. He came to Greene County, Missouri, as a slave and finally was able to buy his freedom with the money he earned whittling ox yokes. Over time, he had saved a down payment of five hundred dollars, and with the money from the yokes, he paid for himself within a year. At some point, he met and fell in love with a slave woman named Matilda, and the couple had a daughter, Amanda Jane. According to Young's account, he purchased his family's freedom in 1847.

The combination of hard work and skilled craftsmanship soon brought Young fame and fortune in building wagons for use on the Santa Fe Trail. His ox-drawn, deep-bedded "Santa Fe" freight wagon could haul up to six thousand pounds of merchandise down the eight hundred-mile trail to New Mexico. In addition to the wagon factory on North Liberty Street in Independence, Young owned a four hundred-acre farm in the Little Blue Valley. By 1860, Hiram Young, was listed in the Independence census as owning thirty thousand dollars' worth of real estate and twenty thousand dollars' worth of personal property.

In 1861, however, when the clouds of the Civil War began to drift across the plains and border conflicts worsened, even this prosperous man began to suffer from racial hatred. Young was forced to abandon his holdings and flee with his family to Ft. Leavenworth, Kansas, where he made his services available to the Union army until the war ended. When he returned to Independence he found his home and shop had been demolished and his personal property confiscated.

Young sued the United States government for damages and loss of his property, but not one to be kept down by circumstances, he built a new shop across the street from the site of his old one. His reputation as a maker of yokes held him in good stead, and his shop continued to attract business. He often shipped orders of four or five hundred yokes to Mexico. Soon, he received government contracts that enabled him to expand his business. After forty-five years of litigation and years after Young's death, his suit against the government was dismissed for lack of evidence.

Hiram Young died in 1882, but his legacy survived the turn of the century. The first African American school founded in Independence was rebuilt on a new location in 1870 and later renamed in his honor. Amanda, his daughter, graduated from Oberlin College and began her teaching career in Independence. For a time she served as principal of the school that bore her father's name. A new Hiram Young School was built in 1935.

One prominent freedman defied the 1847 law that made it illegal to hold schools for blacks or teach blacks within the state. John Berry Meachum wanted to help black children learn to read and write. Born a slave in Virginia, Meachum learned carpentry and finally earned enough money as a carpenter to buy himself and his father. Father and son moved to Kentucky, where Meachum married and then followed his wife's owner to St. Louis. He was able to earn enough money to purchase her freedom and later to open his own business, a barrel factory. Working persistently to free slaves and educate blacks, Meachum founded the earliest black Protestant church in Missouri, the First African Baptist Church of St. Louis. Under the guise of holding a Sunday school, he taught children to read and write. When he learned that word of his activities had reached authorities, he and his supporters opened a school on his steamboat, equipped it with a library, and anchored it in the middle of the Mississippi River, where it was under federal, rather than state, law. He transported his students by boat to the "floating school," which he operated until he died in 1854.

While many whites, both in the North and South, believed that blacks were lazy, incompetent, and unreliable, the achievements of blacks proved them wrong. With skill and determination, free men and women supported themselves in a variety of ways, and some earned substantial fortunes. They worked as stonemasons, stable keepers, blacksmiths, and barbers, among other things, and many opened businesses of their own. Most successful free people in Missouri lived in St. Louis during slavery.

Elizabeth Keckley was born a slave in 1818 in Virginia. Her owner brought her to St. Louis and hired her out as a seamstress. In 1855, with the assistance of some of her customers, she purchased her freedom and that of her son for twelve hundred dollars. She left St. Louis in 1860 and moved to Maryland, settling in Baltimore, where she taught dressmaking. When she moved on to the nation's capital, she began to work for the wives of wealthy men and politicians. In 1861, Mary Todd Lincoln, wife of the president, chose Keckley to make her inaugural gown. The two developed a friendly relationship, and Keckley continued to work for Mrs. Lincoln after President Lincoln was assassinated in 1865.

The friendship ended when Keckley published *Behind the Scenes; or, Thirty Years a Slave and Four Years in the White House,* an autobiography, in 1868. Mrs. Lincoln objected to the intimate details the book revealed about her family's life. Although Keckley lost many of her customers as a result of the controversial book, and her business failed, she had established herself as a prominent member of the Washington, D.C., black community through her charitable work on behalf of African Americans. In 1862, she had founded the Contraband Relief Association to assist former slaves who managed to cross Union lines, and she was one of the founders of the National Association for the Relief of Destitute Women and Children. She lived out the remainder of her life in a home established by that organization. Elizabeth Keckley died in 1907.

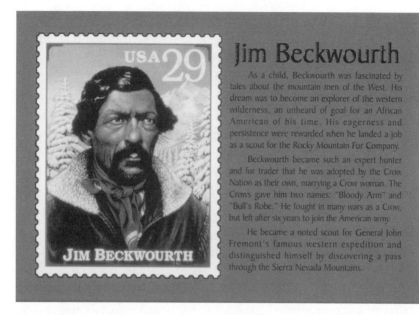

Jim Beckwourth

As a child, Beckwourth was fascinated by tales about the mountain men of the West. His dream was to become an explorer of the western wilderness, an unheard of goal for an African American of his time. His eagerness and persistence were rewarded when he landed a job as a scout for the Rocky Mountain Fur Company.

Beckwourth became such an expert hunter and fur trader that he was adopted by the Crow Nation as their own, marrying a Crow woman. The Crows gave him two names: "Bloody Arm" and "Bull's Robe." He fought in many wars as a Crow, but left after six years to join the American army.

He became a noted scout for General John Fremont's famous western expedition and distinguished himself by discovering a pass through the Sierra Nevada Mountains.

James Beckwourth is one of many black heroes who have been honored with a stamp by the United States Postal Service.

James Beckwourth won fame as an explorer. He had moved to St. Louis with his family around 1806. He was the son of a white Revolutionary War officer and a slave. Under the law, the child of a slave mother was considered a slave. However, within a few years the young Beckwourth was working as an apprentice in a blacksmith shop. Following a quarrel with the blacksmith, he worked in his father's trading post and then went off to work in the lead mines in the area.

In the early 1820s, Beckwourth joined a fur-trapping expedition up the Missouri River and into the Rocky Mountains. He became a well-known explorer and scout and lived with the Crow Indians for many years, eventually becoming a chief. Working as a guide, he discovered a passage through the Sierra Nevada Mountains and led the first expedition through the passage. Composer and songwriter Cecil Williams of Rolla has written that as signs of his great fame, "a town, a mountain, and a pass, still carry Jim Beckwourth's name."

Another explorer, also a black Missourian, was George Bush. After moving from Missouri to the Oregon Territory, he returned several times to lead settlers to the Northwest. In addition, he helped white settlers who migrated there get established. After moving on to what is now Washington State, Bush helped the U.S. government secure its claim to that territory. In recognition of his efforts, his son was chosen to serve in the first legislature to be assembled in the state of Washington.

Although the presence of free blacks in Missouri caused anxiety and fear among some whites in the state, the racial prejudice and oppressive conditions during slavery inspired a spirit of entrepreneurship among Missouri's free black population. By 1850, there were more than 3,500 free blacks in the state, 1,500 of them in St. Louis. While they were technically free, most were still bound by color and condition to the slaves. For the majority, the situation nurtured a relationship of caring and concern that strengthened the ties of community, but some sought to distinguish themselves as "a colored aristocracy."

From the earliest European exploration of the Mississippi valley, the status of children from biracial unions was an issue. When the Americans assumed control of the Louisiana Territory, and the court issued a new "Black Code," "colored" people were defined as "every person other than a negro whose grandfather or grandmother . . . is, or shall have been a negro . . . and every such person who shall have one-fourth or more of negro blood, shall in a like manner be deemed a mulatto." In 1800, Ste. Genevieve's population included eighty-eight people defined as mulattoes, constituting twenty-five percent of the nonwhite community.

The children of black-white unions often had very fair skin and straight or nearly straight hair. Color had a lot to do with the manner in which slaves were treated, and it sometimes affected their freedom. Because of their light skin, mulattoes were sometimes favored and allowed to do less menial work than the darker slaves. Often mulattoes were freed or quickly sold away, especially in cases when their fathers were their owners or related to their owners. This was often necessary to prevent conflicts in an owner's household. As in all cases, the treatment of these slaves depended on the temperament of their owners.

In the case of William Wells Brown, his relationship with his father's family resulted in harsh treatment. His owner's wife resented his presence, which served as a constant reminder of a relationship between her husband's half-brother and a slave. Brown's daughter, in a biography of her famous father, commented on the troublesome dilemma of skin color: "The nearer a slave approaches an Anglo-Saxon in complexion, the more he is abused both by the owner and fellow slaves. The owner flogs him to keep him in his place: and the slaves hate him on account of his being whiter than themselves."

In most cases, mulattoes were subject to the same laws as other African Americans. The case of George Washington of Brookfield was a notable exception to this rule. Washington was the foster son of the Cochrans of Boone County. He was treated as part of the Cochran family and taught to cook, spin, weave, and make his own clothes. He learned to tan cowhides and lay a threshing floor with grain for the animals to tread. Mrs. Cochran read to him from her Bible and taught him hymns. The young man then taught himself to read and to figure. He became a skilled carpenter.

By 1837, George Washington had moved with the Cochran family to Brookfield, where the Cochrans erected a gristmill and a distillery, and Washington and a partner rented a sawmill. In the course of business, he sold some lumber to a white man by the name of Jeremiah Coyle. Coyle refused to pay for the lumber when his bill came due.

Washington won a judgment in the matter. But before he could collect, Coyle had him arrested, claiming that although he was a free man of color, he had no rights in the state of Missouri. Cochran took a petition to the state legislature requesting that his foster son be granted the rights of a citizen since his mother was a white woman of English descent. He stated that Washington was freeborn and of good moral character. By a special act of the legislature, George Washington was given all the privileges and immunities of citizenship except the right to hold office.

It is understandable that the issue of color caused conflict within the slave population. It added to the frustration of the darker slaves, since skin color often determined status in the slave community. The insistence on the "rights of color" was so intense that one group of mulattoes in St. Louis established its own aristocracy. Prominent among the members of this "colored" elite were descendants of Jacques Clamorgan, the West Indian entrepreneur of uncertain parentage who became financially successful as a merchant, fur trader, and land speculator.

Records show that Clamorgan fathered four children by three mulatto women. When he died in 1814, he left these children an estate of only one thousand dollars but claims to many thousands of acres of land; because of conflicting claims over land grants, however, they were forced to fight in the courts for their inheritance for many years, ultimately without much success.

St. Eutrope, one of Clamorgan's sons, married Pelagie Baptiste, the daughter of a slave woman, called Eliza by her mother. He died four years later, and Pelagie remarried, this time to a mulatto of Dutch heritage, Louis Rutgers. She became a major figure of the aristocracy when she acquired large real estate holdings as a result of her second marriage. Madame Rutgers increased her fortunes and became a major landholder in St. Louis in the 1840s, building a home that would become known as the Rutgers mansion. She rented tenements and commercial buildings to white clients and accumulated half a million dollars in assets.

Members of the Colored Aristocracy sought to set themselves apart from other blacks socially and married within their select group, hoping to maintain ties with the white community. In 1858, a year after the Dred Scott decision was handed down, Cyprian Clamorgan, grandson of Jacques, writing an account of "The Colored Aristocracy of St. Louis," noted that "according to the decision of Chief Justice Taney [of the U.S. Supreme Court], a colored man is not a citizen of the United States, and consequently has no political rights under the constitution [but] . . . the colored people of St. Louis command several million dollars; and everyone knows that money, in whose hands soever it may be found, has an influence proportioned to its amount."

Clamorgan could not resist adding that Justice Taney, who had been born on a tobacco plantation in Maryland, "has in this state kindred of a darker hue than himself." Julie Winch, the editor of *The Colored Aristocracy of St. Louis,* reports that Taney's official biographers are "silent on this score."

CHAPTER 3

Let My People Go

When Israel was in Egypt's land / Let my people go.
Oppressed so hard they could not stand / Let my people go.
Go down Moses / 'Way down in Egypt's land,
Tell ol' Pharaoh / Let my people go.

THERE were more than one hundred thousand slaves in Missouri when the Civil War began in 1861. At a special state convention held in March 1861 to decide the question of secession from the Union, the delegates, some of them recent German immigrants who had fled oppression in their country, all opposed secession. After the capture of Jefferson City by the Unionists and the defeat of the State Guards at the Battle of Boonville, Missouri Governor Claiborne Fox Jackson, a slave owner and Confederate sympathizer, fled the state with his wife, children, and slaves. The majority of Missourians served on the side of the Union during the conflict, but guerrilla "bushwhackers" waged war against Union sympathizers throughout the 1860s and afterward.

The issue of blacks serving in the Union army was hotly debated. Slaveholders were generally opposed to the enrollment of slaves, but antislavery factions argued strongly for their enlistment. The slaves, of course, had everything at stake. They realized that enlistment alone meant their own personal freedom and could mean the freedom of their brothers and sisters if the Union won the war. They were eager to serve, and the Union army needed the manpower. On July 31,

First Sergeant Nelson Bergamise, twenty-four, of
New Franklin enlisted at Boonville and served in
Company C, Sixty-second United States Colored
Troops during the Civil War. While in Texas, the men
of the Sixty-second and Sixty-fifth Colored Troops
made plans to build a school to train black teachers.
Researchers at the Department of Natural Resources
determined that Bergamise and others in the company were slaves, whose owners received up to three
hundred dollars in compensation when they enlisted.
(Lincoln Collection, Page Library, Lincoln University, Jefferson City, Mo., courtesy Missouri Department of Natural Resources)

1863, President Abraham Lincoln ordered that able-bodied black men between the ages of twenty and forty-five be allowed to enlist.

The federal government paid slaveholders three hundred dollars if a slave volunteered for service and a one hundred dollar bounty for each slave enlisted. The money, and the fact that when slaves were signed up fewer whites were required to serve, won over some slaveholders.

The first black Missouri regiment was recruited at Schofield Barracks in St. Louis in the summer of 1863. Ultimately, there were seven black Missouri regiments in the service of the Union. Since the discrimination they suffered in civilian life was still evident in military life, most of these soldiers served in noncombatant companies, performing manual labor, with some serving in the infantry. Some, including Peter Paul Tolton, died before having an opportunity to fight.

Many black soldiers were actively engaged in several contests, notably in Tennessee, Texas, Louisiana, and Alabama. Among these were the Sixty-second and Sixty-fifth U.S. Colored Infantries, who pooled their money after the war ended to found Lincoln Institute in Jefferson City, now Lincoln University. Black men served in many roles—from cooks to spies—and women often served as nurses, cooks, and laundresses. After the war, more than 170 noncombatant officers and privates, members of the Sixty-sixth Colored Infantry, died of cholera in 1866. Their bodies were interred at Jefferson Barracks National Cemetery in St. Louis.

Other black Missourians served in the regiments of other states such as those of Kansas and Iowa. Some slaves used the war as an opportunity to escape slavery and found work in Union camps. In all, some eight thousand black Missouri soldiers served in the Union's cause in the Civil War.

Although President Abraham Lincoln had issued the Emancipation Proclamation on January 1, 1863, it freed only those slaves in states or parts of states that were in rebellion against the Union. The Missouri State Legislature passed "An Ordinance Abolishing Slavery in Missouri" in 1865, the first state in the nation to do so, and Governor Thomas Fletcher signed a "Proclamation of Freedom" on January 11, 1865. The enslaved in Missouri were finally free.

Slavery had been a cruel way of life. The institution inflicted immeasurable harm on both the bodies and the psyches of the children of African descent. It has left a permanent blot on Missouri's history, but out of the slave condition came many of the valued customs and traditions that remain dear to the hearts of African Americans today.

In some ways it was a time to forget, but in other ways it was a time to remember. They laughed, they sang, they prayed, and they cried with joy. The long, dark night of slavery was over, and now they were free, free at last. But freedom for Missouri's slaves, however welcome, brought with it new problems. The newly emancipated were overjoyed by the knowledge that they were free from the whip and free to go wherever they chose. But without money, property, or education, they faced a world nearly as hostile as the one they were leaving behind.

Many freed slaves left their former owners' homes as soon as they got word of their freedom. Some set out in search of families from whom they had been separated. Some just ran, not knowing where they were going but willing to risk anything rather than remain with their former owners. Freedom called them, but it could not be a reality until they felt free, and they could not feel free until their own legs carried them away from the land on which they had been slaves.

While most fled from the farms to the cities, some stayed behind, in their old homes, biding their time, looking for places to live and work. Some former slave owners, having lost their free labor force, were bitter and unwilling to lend aid or assistance to prepare their former slaves for their new way of life. Others accepted the reality of emancipation and offered to pay for their work. Some granted former slaves a small portion of land in exchange for services. The men, when they could find work, became farmhands or laborers. The women were primarily household servants.

Although determined to carve out a life for themselves, the newly freed Missourians were often anxious and fearful. They drew on the customs and traditions of their past to forge a future in which they hoped to enjoy full participation in the democratic way of life. One of the first challenges most of them faced was choosing a full name. Many slaves had been assigned a first name by their owners but had no family or last name. Most had been given common names like Mary or Susie for females and Jim or Bob for males. Catholics often had names of saints—Peter, Paul, or Joseph. Now, as free citizens, they would need last names as well. Some chose names of prominent people like George Washington; some just added the last names of their former owners to the names they had; and some took descriptive names like "Freeman" or "Carpenter." Many also rejected the term *Negro,* which they felt was a designation associated with slavery. Now, in their freedom, they chose to be called *colored.*

Another problem arose when the ex-slaves tried to establish family ties. Since slaves had not been allowed to legally marry, husbands and wives were joined only by common law. The Freedmen's Bureau, which had been established by the federal government, sent agents to Missouri in 1865 to help the former slaves build new lives. In addition to helping them meet the needs of everyday life, such as finding food and shelter and establishing schools, the agents also performed a variety of other services. For example, the Missouri legislature passed a law after the Civil War, giving former slaves a year to legalize marriages, and the bureau's agents assisted many couples in accomplishing this. The road to freedom would not prove easy to travel, but compared to the indignities and cruelties of life in bondage, no path was too difficult now.

* * *

Pennytown in Saline County became a thriving community of freed blacks. (Collection of Rose Nolen)

After emancipation, the most visible evidence of the strong tradition of community ties was the all-black towns and communities in which African Americans banded together in their efforts to survive and, eventually, to flourish. Some settlements grew up on the edges of established towns, and others were "intentional communities," specifically for the newly freed. Joseph Penny, a free black man from Kansas, founded Pennytown on land he purchased in Saline County in 1870. In its heyday it boasted two hundred residents.

Citizens of Pennytown raised their own food and had their own blacksmith, school, and church, and they shared responsibilities. Older women in the community cared for the children when parents found jobs in neighboring towns. Eventually most residents of Pennytown moved to towns or cities. The last resident, Francis Spears, died in 1979, but the Pennytown Freewill Baptist Church, which has been on the National Register of Historic Places since 1988, still stands, and the community cemetery is undisturbed. Each year, descendants of the founders and residents gather for a homecoming.

Eldridge in Laclede County developed when a town grew up around land owned by Alfred Eldridge, a former Tennessee slave, in the 1880s. Bill Driver, a famous Missouri fiddler, was born in Eldridge, the son of an early settler.

Shortly after Emancipation, former slaves in Boone County settled an area called Three Creeks, named for its location near Bass, Bonne Femme, and Turkey Creeks. Former slaves became landowners in the community by working on land belonging to their former owners. By 1900, sixty-six blacks owned farms in the community. Between 1867 and 1930 blacks bought more than four thousand acres in Three Creeks. Many later lost their land through foreclosures, failure to make wills, delinquent taxes, and other problems, but in 1950 African Americans still owned half of the land in the area. Log Providence Baptist Church remains on the site of Three Creeks. Many members still commute from Columbia to attend services there, and many descendants of Three Creeks families attend the annual homecoming celebration.

Little Africa, a tract of wooded land near Louisiana in Pike County, which, according to legend, had served as a hideaway for runaway slaves, later became a settlement. The last family in Little Africa left in the 1930s or 1940s. In the Westport area of Kansas City, in Jackson County, a small black settlement took shape on land granted to African Americans by their former owners. These families built substantial homes and developed and maintained a strong neighborhood presence for nearly a hundred years.

Today historians are documenting the achievements of many of the all-black communities, urban and rural, large and small, that grew up across Missouri in the nineteenth and twentieth centuries, such as Kinloch in St. Louis County and the Cave community in Callaway County. Some have faded into history, but both those that remain and those that have disappeared represent another effort by African Americans to lay claim to a part of the state they helped to build and in which they wanted to establish communities of their own. Despite facing overwhelming poverty, racial hatred, and systematic oppression, freed blacks clung firmly to the tradition of community that had nurtured them during the years of slavery.

The custom of an extended family caring for the old, sick, and orphaned, and the willingness of individuals to share their meager portions strengthened the community as members moved forward to better their lot. They established their own churches and schools. They formed their own social, civic, and fraternal organizations, banding together in the cause of mutual aid and self-help. The lessons of slavery combined with the indifference former owners now showed them taught them that if the race was going to survive and flourish, those who were better off had to reach out and lift up their fellow citizens.

As early as 1865, black citizens of Columbia organized an African court, where differences among themselves could be fairly settled. The unofficial court consisted of three judges and a sheriff. By 1867, leaders had formed the First African Benevolent Society of Columbia to serve the aged, the infirm, and the destitute. The membership fee was two dollars, and the monthly dues were fifty cents. Members of the black community also established a temperance society.

While the black communities struggled valiantly to relieve the distress of their members, in March of 1879, blacks, first in St. Louis and later in Kansas City, were called on to extend their arms further to assist a mass movement of black emigrants from southern states who unexpectedly arrived on their doorsteps. The large number of migrants who fled the South after the war, some under the leadership of ex-slave Benjamin "Paps" Singleton, became known as the Exodusters.

Singleton had been a cabinetmaker and coffinmaker in Ten-

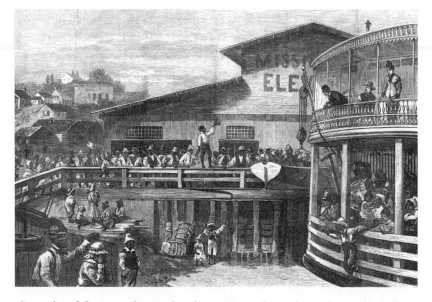

Crowds of former slaves, hoping to travel north, wait on the wharf at Vicksburg. (State Historical Society of Missouri, Columbia)

nessee. After watching his fellow former slaves struggle in vain to acquire land to farm, he organized efforts to convince them that their future lay not in the South, but in Kansas, where there was land available to "homestead." In 1870, a small party traveled to Kansas to scout the location and consider the possibility of migration. They returned with a positive report about homesteading activities going on there. A few families migrated and agreed that circumstances were favorable. In 1873, Singleton explored southeastern Kansas and found that lands formerly occupied by the Cherokee Nation would be well suited as homesteads for Tennessee blacks. By 1878, more families had migrated, and the former slave leader had formed the Singleton Colony in Morris County, Kansas. It was incorporated in 1879. Singleton passed out circulars offering to lead parties who would migrate to his colony, held mass meetings to spread the word, and sponsored festivals and picnics to raise money for migration expenses.

In March 1879, the first group of Exodusters arrived in St. Louis, catching that community totally by surprise. Over the next four months, more than six thousand of these migrants would make their way up the Mississippi and land in St. Louis on the first stage of their journey to Kansas. Unfortunately, many had exhausted their funds getting to St. Louis, and families were often forced to sell their household goods to complete the trip. News of the Exodusters' plight reached Charleston Tandy, one of St. Louis's most prominent black politicians. He appealed to the Mullanphy Emigrant Relief Board, administered by the city of St. Louis, for help. His request was turned down, but Tandy managed to raise one hundred dollars from among the board's membership, which he used to find lodging for the migrants in the homes of black families.

As migrants continued to pour into the city, a mass meeting was called in the black community, and a Colored Refugee Relief Board was formed. Black organizations and churches added their support to the task of feeding and housing the migrants. Most white St. Louisans refused to cooperate in the effort, but word eventually spread around the country, and sympathetic people began sending contributions to help. In less than a month, black St. Louis leaders raised nearly three thousand dollars' worth of goods and services for the migrants, enabling many to complete their journey to Kansas. The migrants who arrived in Kansas City found help from the Reverend B. B. Watson, of the African Methodist Episcopal Church, who initiated a relief effort that was then supported by the city's mayor.

This episode demonstrates the determination of Missouri's African Americans to carry on the traditions of self-help and mutual aid that had been fostered by the conditions of slavery, even to extending assistance to total strangers and even when their own circumstances were not much better than those of the people they were helping.

Black women took the lead in forming organizations intended to help families and promote moral values during the trials and tribulations of the late nineteenth century. A shelter for homeless black children opened in 1883 in Kansas City. The home later became known as the Niles Home for Children. The St. Louis Colored Orphan's Home, founded in 1888 and incorporated in 1889, provided care in a group living situation for neglected and dependent children. A home for the aged was established shortly thereafter. In 1890 black women in Jefferson City established a Woman's Christian Temperance Union. In St. Joseph and St. Louis, women formed F. E. W. Harper leagues. These leagues were named in honor of Frances Ellen Watkins Harper, a writer and social activist in Philadelphia, Pennsylvania. Harper participated in the abolitionist, woman's suffrage, and temperance movements. Black women organized a Women's Club of Jefferson City and the Phyllis Wheatley Club of St. Louis. The National Association of Colored Women's Clubs made its debut in St. Louis in 1890. Its purpose was to bring women's clubs across the state together under one umbrella.

Many women who saw the needs within their communities and responded to them were responsible for founding and supporting organizations to aid their people. Lucinda Lewis Haskell's mother was a former slave. She instilled a desire to achieve in her daughter and inspired her to "become somebody." Haskell might well have believed that she had accomplished the goal her mother set for her when she became one of the first graduates of Lincoln Institute. But as it turned out, this was only to be the beginning of her life of service.

Haskell taught for a time in Jefferson City, then she and her mother moved to St. Louis. Joining a group of like-minded black women, Haskell became one of her community's first volunteer social workers. Recognizing the need to provide care for the community's orphans, she helped organize a club under the leadership of Sarah Newton. The club was responsible for establishing the St. Louis Colored Orphan's Home in 1888 in an abandoned home for soldiers.

Although she was by this time the mother of five children, Haskell, along with fellow club members, made quilts, sheets, and other linens for the orphan's home, shopped for the children's food, and appealed for donations from the public. When the group's efforts paid off, the women moved on to organize a home for the elderly. Later these women organized a chapter of the Colored Women's Federated Clubs, which brought black women's clubs together to work toward a common purpose.

Another black woman who worked to help others was Josephine Silone Yates, who came to Missouri in 1881 to begin a teaching career at Lincoln Institute. Born in New York and educated in Philadelphia and Rhode Island, she married in 1889 and moved to Kansas City. There, she wrote for the black press, urging the betterment of blacks, and began to work actively in community service. She helped found the Women's League of Kansas City, an organization of black women, and served as its president. This group helped to establish homes and schools for unemployed young black women and ultimately founded a branch of the Young Women's Christian Association (YWCA) for black women and girls. She was elected president of the National Association of Colored Women in 1901 and returned to teach at Lincoln Institute in 1902, where she continued to write articles on racial issues. Yates, who also taught at Lincoln High School in Kansas City, died in 1912. An arts and charity club bearing her name continues to flourish in Sedalia.

In rural Missouri farm laborers often worked merely for food and shelter. In towns they found work as laborers or cooks and in other menial jobs but had to find their own lodging.

Josephine Yates, one of Lincoln University's best-known teachers in the late nineteenth and early twentieth centuries, was president of the National Association of Colored Women's Clubs from 1901 to 1906. (Lincoln Collection, Page Library, Lincoln University, Jefferson City, Mo., courtesy State Historical Society of Missouri, Columbia)

They heard of better opportunities in the cities, and by 1890 nearly half of the black population in the state had moved to St. Louis or Kansas City. Having hoped to improve their lives, most soon found themselves crowded into already heavily populated enclaves. Because they had little or no money, these new residents were forced to live in rundown houses or tenements in the poorest sections of the city.

In Kansas City, blacks settled in the northeast part of the city, in areas known as Belvidere and Hicks Hollows. They lived in shanties along dirt streets or alleys cluttered with debris and crowded with bars that city officials ignored. Water mains and sanitary sewers either did not exist or were not maintained. Many blacks who had originally settled in the West Bottoms of the city relocated into the North End, causing even greater congestion. Crime rates were high, since crime in the area was virtually ignored by the police. Jobs were scarce. Most blacks worked as common laborers and had difficulty finding permanent jobs. Women worked as housekeepers, maids, and laundresses. The situation was much the same in St. Louis, where blacks were crowded together along the northwest fringe of downtown in an area known as Clabber Alley. Those who remained in the smaller towns also frequently lived crowded together in sections of town that were largely ignored by officials. In Jefferson City, the black settlement was called Hog Alley, and for many residents there seemed no way to escape the filth and squalor in the area.

One notable exception occurred in Greene County in southwest Missouri, where blacks made up one-fourth of the population. Katherine Lederer of Southwest Missouri State University has documented their achievement in developing a rich cultural and social environment by the turn of the twentieth century. Before 1900, three blacks served on the Springfield City Council, and blacks also served on the school board. In addition, blacks owned several prosperous businesses in the city, including the largest grocery store. As their prosperity grew, the hostility of some whites toward the former slaves increased. In 1906 an angry crowd burst into the Springfield jail, pulled three men outside, and lynched them. Two of the men had been accused of raping a white woman; the other man was simply being held in the jail at the time.

The violence spread into the black neighborhood, and hundreds of residents fled the city within a few days of the lynchings. During the late nineteenth and early twentieth centuries, the outbreaks of violence became a reign of terror. Between 1889 and 1918, fifty-one blacks were lynched in Missouri. In response, the first half of the new century saw the establishment of many branches of the National Association for the Advancement of Colored People (NAACP) and witnessed the expansion of the National Negro Federated Women's Clubs. The Young Men's Christian Association and its companion program for women gained footholds in Kansas City. The first Grand Lodge of Free and Accepted Ancient York Masons, which had been organized in St. Louis in 1865, opened a Masonic home near Hannibal to care for elderly and impoverished Masons and their orphans. By 1911, Kansas City's Afro-American Investment and Employment Company had found jobs for over six thousand men and women in that community.

CHAPTER 4

Building New Lives

W HILE some black children had learned to read and write from people like John Berry Meachum, most of those who celebrated their freedom at the end of the Civil War were illiterate. So schools were among the first institutions former slaves wanted to establish. They knew that to make the most of their freedom their children had to learn to read and write. In a spirit of community building, a newly freed people determined to uplift one another by making education available to all of their people.

Agents of the Freedmen's Bureau arrived in Missouri in 1865 to assist in the effort to set up "colored" schools, but progress was slow. Many town and community officials were not willing to invest in education for black children. For most former slaves, opportunities to learn were no better than they had been during slavery. The lack of education for black children was one of the problems that had led an assembly of several prominent black men to form the Missouri Equal Rights League in St. Louis in 1865. This organization was a branch of the National Equal Rights League, which had been founded in 1864.

The Missouri Equal Rights League set up a seven-member committee whose duties included finding ways and means to educate black children. They hired a black lawyer, John Langston of Ohio, to tour the state and assess the situation. James Milton Turner, an eloquent speaker and secretary of the league, also became an outspoken advocate for schools for African Americans. The Missouri Constitution of 1865 required school boards to establish and maintain schools for blacks if there were fifteen children in a township between the ages of five and twenty-one. However, this law was enforced haphazardly. In 1869, the Freedmen's Bureau hired Turner to assist in setting up black schools throughout the state. The state superintendent of schools also appointed him to serve in that capacity. Turner was well qualified to assume this role. Born a slave in St. Louis, he had gained his freedom in 1844 when he was four years old; his owner had emancipated the young boy along with his mother, Hannah. After attending school in St. Louis, Turner had gone on to Oberlin College in Ohio.

For seven months in 1869–1870, he traveled across the state, investigating educational opportunities available for blacks. He faced hostility in many areas; citizens in Liberty and Independence threatened to lynch him. Townships in southeast Missouri were particularly resistant to educating blacks.

Frequently, he found that officials had undercounted students in an effort to avoid starting schools. In all, Turner recorded that he had traveled close to ten thousand miles, raised several thousand dollars, directed the building of eight schools, and opened thirty-two schools within the state. His employment with the Freedmen's Bureau ended in 1870 when the organization cut back its services in the former slave states.

But the drive for African American schools did not stop. Black people continued to work in their own communities to establish their own schools. As Turner accepted a job as a teacher at Lincoln Institute in Jefferson City, black citizens from Kansas City to St. Louis and from the Bootheel to northern Missouri continued to fight for their right to education. Although there were only fifty-nine schools for blacks in the state by 1869, according to one report, the tradition of working as a community had its impact, and black leaders continued to press for equal access to learning.

Most black communities in Missouri named their early colored schools after presidents, abolitionists, or prominent black leaders. Schools were commonly named for President Abraham Lincoln, abolitionists Charles Sumner and Frederick Douglass, scientist George Washington Carver, educator Booker T. Washington, poet Paul Laurence Dunbar, and freedom fighter Crispus Attucks of Revolutionary War fame. Like other rural schools of the time, schools for African American children were usually one-room buildings with one teacher for students in grades one through eight. As the demands for education gained momentum, new schools were built or rooms were added. Textbooks and teaching supplies were usually hand-me-downs from white schools, and many of the early teachers were poorly educated.

It was under these conditions that Sedalia established Lincoln School in a two-room building soon after the Civil War. According to James Milton Turner, who visited the school in 1869, agents from the Freedmen's Bureau had found it to be poorly organized and run by an incompetent teacher who practiced the liberal use of a cowhide whip to punish children.

The most serious problems faced by the pioneers of the early black school movement in Missouri was the critical shortage of blacks who were qualified to teach when the Civil War ended. Since few black faculty were available, some white teachers, mainly from Oberlin College in Ohio, offered to fill the gap. This effort was met with some dissatisfaction in many black communities. Leaders marshaled their few political resources and set out to remedy this situation.

School advocate James Milton Turner and St. Louis political activist Reverend Moses Dickson called for a gathering of black leaders in Jefferson City in January 1870. The purpose of the meeting was to encourage blacks to pressure the state legislature to provide financial assistance to Lincoln Institute to train black teachers. The institute, which had begun with only two students in 1866, in a dilapidated building in Jefferson City, was struggling to survive.

A month after the Jefferson City meeting, the Missouri

General Assembly passed a law that granted Lincoln Institute five thousand dollars a year, provided it turned its facilities into a school for training black teachers. Lincoln was also required to raise fifteen thousand dollars in cash, land, buildings or a combination of those assets. The institute's board of trustees accepted the challenge.

For the men of the Sixty-second and Sixty-fifth U.S. Colored Infantries, it had all begun with a dream. For Richard Foster, a white native of New Hampshire and graduate of Dartmouth College, who agreed to help these men fulfill their dream, it turned out to be somewhat of a nightmare in the beginning. Black soldiers serving at Benton Barracks during the Civil War had an opportunity to learn to read and write through a program launched by the Western Sanitary Commission, a philanthropic organization in St. Louis. Under the leadership of their white officers they continued their classes at night. The soldiers began to dream of a school for blacks in Missouri where they could continue their education at the end of the war. They persuaded Foster, who served as a first lieutenant with the Sixty-second, to start the school provided they could raise the needed funds. The Sixty-second managed to raise five thousand dollars, and the Sixty-fifth contributed another thirteen hundred.

After leaving the army, Foster attempted to start the school in St. Louis. No help was forthcoming, and so he moved to Jefferson City. Even in the new location he found little financial support. In a biographical sketch of Foster, in his history of Lincoln University, Antonio Holland explains that when Foster asked the black Methodist Church for help, he was refused because the teacher was white. He turned to the white Methodists, who refused because the students were black. But he found support among some German radicals in the capital and others, and he persevered.

Following a rocky beginning, the school began to fill with students. Foster, who served as first principal and teacher, was

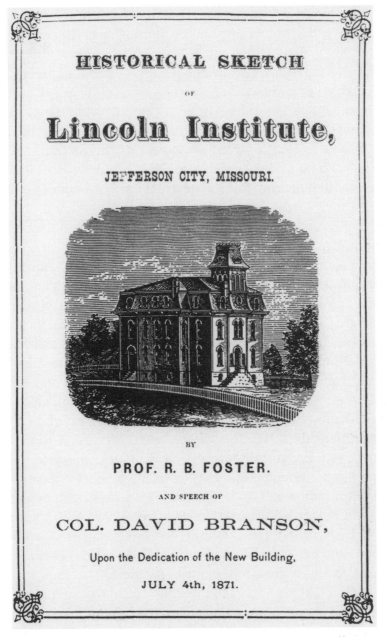

First Building at Lincoln. (Lincoln Collection, Page Library, Lincoln University, Jefferson City, Mo.)

soon forced to hire another teacher to assist him. The institute opened with a preparatory and a normal department. When the state finally granted aid to the school, several organizations and individuals contributed to the effort, including the legendary Jesse James. Judge Arnold Krekel, who had served as president of the 1865 Missouri State Constitutional Convention that developed the "Ordinance Abolishing Slavery in Missouri," was a strong supporter of the institute. With the assistance of Jefferson City black businessman Howard Barnes, Lincoln was able to construct its first building on the site of the present campus in 1871. Still, financial problems continued, and Foster often had to teach in the Jefferson City schools to survive.

Lincoln School in Sedalia was enlarged to a four-room building in 1879 and underwent a major transition in 1906, when Christopher Columbus Hubbard became its principal. Hubbard, a native of Glasgow, had earned several degrees from Lincoln Institute and was considered one of the finest black educators in the state. When he took the helm, Lincoln School was in a poorly equipped frame building and had a staff of six teachers. All grades attended the school, although initially only two years of academic work was offered by the high school. In 1916, the school began offering a four-year high school curriculum, and the class of 1915 returned to the school and graduated in 1917. In 1926 Hubbard oversaw the building of an annex to house the high school. The two fireproof buildings included twenty-one classrooms, a gymnasium-auditorium, a cafeteria, a shop for industrial arts, a home economics department, a library, and an office. During his tenure, the staff grew to seventeen teachers.

C. C. Hubbard was the moving force that transformed Lincoln School from an unclassified school into a state-accredited high school and a member of the North Central Association of Colleges and Secondary Schools. Under his guidance, the school became one of the most highly respected

Christoper Columbus Hubbard, longtime principal of Hubbard School. (State Historical Society of Missouri, Columbia)

in the state. Students from nearby communities such as Marshall, Warrensburg, Knob Noster, and Tipton came to the school by bus until 1955.

In appreciation of his administrative abilities, the Sedalia Board of Education renamed Lincoln in 1943. It became the C. C. Hubbard School. A twenty-five-acre plot near the school, which Sarah Smith Cotton, a daughter of Sedalia's founder, had donated as a park for colored citizens, was also renamed for Hubbard.

Among the principal's most loyal and faithful admirers were the benefactors of his efforts—the African American schoolchildren of Sedalia. In dedicating its school annual, the *Lincolnian,* to him, the class of 1927 wrote, "Through his rare

humor and wit, he takes the dryness out of what would otherwise be ordinary school life, and puts into it a little of the sun-
nyside of life." In May 1937, the school paper, the *Lincoln
School Philosophian,* stated, "Whatever success has come to
Lincoln School has come through the leadership and persistent efforts of our Principal, Prof. C. C. Hubbard." Christopher
Columbus Hubbard served as principal of Hubbard School
until his death on May 23, 1947.

Education was so important to blacks that most community
life revolved around the black schools. Parents, teachers, and
other members of the community were actively involved in
school affairs. The school served as a community center as
well as an educational institution. It was a place to hold meetings, share information and concerns, and provide cultural
enrichment.

In addition to their academic activities, most Missouri
black schools prided themselves on their music departments.
Both vocal and instrumental music were valued parts of the
school curriculum. Students considered it a high privilege to
be chosen to participate in a school's chorus or band. Smaller
vocal groups of various sizes also flourished. Schools frequently presented a variety of musical programs, from classical to popular music, for students and the community.

Competition among black schools for academic excellence,
sports, and music was keen. Elementary schools that were
located in towns near one another had their students compete
in spelling bees and track and field events. High school students competed for state honors in shorthand, typing, music,
football, basketball, and oratory.

Hubbard High School closed its doors in 1967. Until the
end, it remained the center of black social and cultural life in
the Sedalia community. The school-community relationship
that existed in Sedalia was typical of that in towns and cities
across the state. The closing of the black schools represented
the end of an important era in African American life in

George R. Smith College. (State Historical Society of Missouri, Columbia)

Missouri and the first step in a new journey toward equality of opportunity in Missouri.

George R. Smith College for Negroes, a Methodist school in Sedalia, opened its doors in January 1894 with an enrollment of fifty-seven students. The Freedmen's Aid and Southern Education Society of the Methodist Church built the school on twenty-four acres of land donated by the daughters of Sedalia's founder, George R. Smith. The four-story building, constructed of red brick with stone trim, cost forty thousand dollars. It had sixty-two rooms, including a chapel that could seat four hundred, male and female dormitories for seventy-five boarding students, the president's suite of rooms, apartments for teachers, a dining hall and kitchen, a library, a music hall, and numerous other facilities. It was heated by steam and lit by gas and electricity.

The college offered eight courses of study: classical, philosophical, scientific, a normal department to prepare teachers, commercial, English, musical, and industrial. To graduate with a bachelor of arts degree, a student had to complete 126 hours of credit. The college also offered three, three-year college preparatory courses. It soon had girls' and boys' basketball teams and a football team in addition to its academic program. The first president of the school was the Reverend P. A. Cool, ex-president of Wiley University, in Marshall, Texas.

The college had an extensive musical program. Ragtime musician Scott Joplin was probably its most famous student. Joplin studied harmony and music theory during his residence in Sedalia. Other prominent graduates of the school were Homer G. Phillips, a black lawyer and activist in St. Louis, and Percy Turner, a physician in Kansas City. By the time it was destroyed by fire on April 26, 1925, the college had graduated more than three thousand students. Many of them pursued teaching careers in Missouri schools.

Another historical school involved in higher education for blacks was Stowe, a teacher's college in St. Louis, which was established in 1890. The school developed from the normal department of Sumner High School in "The Ville," a prosperous African American neighborhood in St. Louis. The college's name honored the writer and antislavery activist Harriet Beecher Stowe, whose novel *Uncle Tom's Cabin,* expressing her outrage over the Fugitive Slave Law of 1850, gained worldwide success. Following desegregation, Stowe merged with Harris, a teacher's school for whites, in 1954. Harris-Stowe became part of the state university system in 1979.

The Bartlett Agricultural and Industrial School in Chariton County had a different mission, and it remains one of the lesser-known educational institutions founded in Missouri by an African American. Nathaniel Bruce established the school

Dr. Percy C. Turner graduated from Meharry Medical College in Nashville and practiced medicine in Kansas City for thirty-seven years. He was the founder of Lake Placid, "A Recreational Center for Colored People," established in Morgan and Benton Counties near Stover in the 1930s. In a 1963 interview by Lucille Bluford, for the *Kansas City Call,* he said, "We could find no place in Jackson County that would accept Negroes, so we turned elsewhere." (Collection of Leonard Pryor)

The 1953–1954 Dalton Vocational School Chapter of New Farmers of America from the 1954 *Blue Jay*. (Collection of Eliot Battle)

in 1907. Bruce was born around 1868 on a farm in Virginia. While attending public school, he worked with his father, a former slave, on the farm. He went to Shaw's Normal and Industrial High School in Raleigh, North Carolina, and later earned a bachelor's degree from Shaw University. He also attended Bates College in Maine, Hampton Institute in Virginia, and Tuskegee in Alabama.

Bruce came to Missouri to accept a job as principal of a high school for blacks in St. Joseph. His major interest was in agriculture, and his goal was to establish his own school using Booker T. Washington's Tuskegee Institute as a model. He operated his first school from a log barn near Dalton on land owned by a former slave, renting land in the Missouri River bottoms for his crops. Unfortunately, floods destroyed his first two crops. With the help of some Missouri supporters, he was able to move out of the flood area and buy land on which

Eliot Battle, who received a B.S. and an M.S. degree from Tuskegee Institute in Alabama, served as principal of Dalton School during its last year of operation. His wife, Muriel, served as secretary. The family lived on the campus. The Battles moved to Columbia in 1956 and became very active in community service. (*Blue Jay,* 1954, courtesy Eliot Battle)

to erect his first permanent building. He named the school after one of its benefactors, Judge James Bartlett. The school's operating expenses and teachers' salaries were paid by private donations and money raised from crops and livestock.

The school finally gained recognition for Bruce and his pupils when its corn crop earned a *Missouri Ruralist* trophy in 1913 and second place nationally in the Panama-Pacific International Exposition. From its first year the school sponsored the annual Missouri–Midwestern States Negro Farmers' and Farm Women's conference, which attracted blacks from throughout the state. By 1920, Bartlett had more than two hundred students.

Following years of agitation, Nathaniel Bruce achieved his goal of having his school serve as an experimental farm for the training of black youth. In 1923 the school donated fifty acres to the state for the development of his model farm and the general assembly appropriated fifteen thousand dollars for the development and administration of the program at Dalton under the supervision of the University of Missouri's college of agriculture. The school was renamed Dalton Vocational School. In 1924, Bruce left the school he had founded to become state inspector of Negro schools. And in 1929 control of Dalton was transferred to Lincoln University. Dalton continued to educate African Americans until 1956, when its doors closed.

The church was another building block for establishing new black communities. People unleashed from slavery welcomed the bonds of religion and treasured the freedom to worship in their own style. The first black church in Missouri was the First African Baptist Church of St. Louis, which former slave John Berry Meachum founded in 1825, forming it from a congregation assembled in 1818 by two Baptist missionaries. Meachum led the congregation to form a separate branch, and following his ordination, he became its first pastor.

The African Methodist Episcopal denomination had already made inroads in St. Louis by 1840 and the following year established its first church in a log cabin with the Reverend Hiram Revels as the pastor. Reverend Revels later moved to Mississippi and became the first black to serve a full term in the U.S. Senate, chosen in 1870 to occupy the seat formerly held by Jefferson Davis, president of the Confederate States of America.

Shortly after emancipation, black centers of worship sprang up all across the state. People worshiped wherever they could gather, in brush arbors, homes, or in open fields, until churches could be built. By 1880, the black Baptists alone had created 150 churches and had 10,000 members. Methodists, African

Methodists, and Presbyterians had also formed congregations. By 1926 there were 645 black churches in Missouri with a total membership of over 80,000.

Many black congregations quickly fell back upon their African traditions, combining them with aspects of the European tradition and continuing the worship styles they had adopted in the invisible churches. Although the bonds of slavery had been loosened, the barriers of color discrimination still plagued every aspect of their lives, and the majority of the liberated slaves found comfort in taking their frustrations to God. They were confident that the God who had seen them through the long, dark night of slavery would deliver them from the cruelties and injustices they still suffered. The Christianity to which they had been converted found new expression among an oppressed people whose lives were still burdened by racial hatred. Within that context, the black church evolved into more than just a center of worship. It became the community's benevolent society, employment office, and its civic and political arm, because it was the place where the congregants shared their concerns.

Still, the often stomping, shouting, and frenzied fits of religious ecstacy that characterized black worship did little to make it more acceptable to whites. Most white Christians considered this style of worship primitive. Many educated blacks also shunned such activities, considering the spirited worship services an embarrassment. As Langston Hughes wrote in "High to Low,"

> God knows
> We have our troubles, too—
> One trouble is you. . . .
> The way you shout out in church.

The more educated the blacks, the more they tended to follow the worship styles of their former owners.

But the tradition begun in slavery, through which the songs told the story of the slave experience, continued to express the spiritual status of the former slaves. Just as the Negro spiritual had served the needs of a rural people in bondage, a new sound was born that expressed the needs of an urbanized, emancipated people, struggling under the burden of discrimination. Now unhampered by the restrictions of an artificial decorum placed on them by the slave owners, they proclaimed their religious fervor boldly. In loud, unrestrained voices, they pleaded with God, they petitioned God, and they professed their faith with a new "joyful noise." By the 1920s this new music, known as the historic black gospel, had become the new song of the church. It was called gospel because, unlike the words in the spirituals, the lyrics were primarily taken from the first four books of the New Testament. Driven by the music, the worship experience took on other new forms. Camp meetings were replaced by revivals, and traveling preachers became known as evangelists.

The traditions of religious worship captured the essence of the new age, but not all of the freed people chose to spend their free time reading the Bible or attending church. With the collapse of slavery, conditions in Missouri had gradually changed. Despite the restrictions that remained and frequent threats of white violence, blacks in Missouri had tasted the first fruits of freedom. They were free to travel, free to gather, more free to exchange stories, share experiences, and explore possibilities. They had their own establishments and institutions where they could express their feelings freely. Outside white control, they were free to reinvent themselves. They were now "colored" people.

Some pursued the pleasures of the flesh. Bars and bawdy houses competed with churches for patrons. Now music began to develop other stories and set the tone for years to come. In the 1890s the African musical rhythms that had fueled the Negro spiritual joined with European musical styles and spread from the black church into saloons and parlors to create a new form of African American musical expression. It originated in St. Louis and became known as ragtime.

Black businessman "Honest" John Turpin's Silver Dollar Saloon, located in the Chestnut Valley district of St. Louis, was a gathering spot for traveling black musicians who made their way up the Mississippi River. Chestnut Valley was lined with sporting houses and saloons, in which musicians could find work as cafe pianists. Turpin's saloon was especially popular for its piano contests, where the young musicians could test their skills against those of their peers. Combining the African sounds of "patting Juba," spirituals, shouts, and hollers with the European polkas and waltzes, or "ragging the melodies" as it was called, was a favorite pastime among the musicians. These jam sessions were known as "cutting contests," with the musicians cutting one another out for a chance to show off their talents. Turpin's son Tom composed the first ragtime piece, the "Harlem Rag," in 1892. According to music historian Edward A. Berlin, ragtime was introduced to the general public at the Chicago World's Fair the following year.

Scott Joplin, who came to be known as the "King of Ragtime," had arrived on the St. Louis scene around 1885. Joplin, the son of a former slave, was born in Texarkana, Texas. Until the early 1900s, he made his home in both St. Louis and Sedalia. It was in Sedalia that he published his famous "Maple Leaf Rag" in 1899. With its publication, ragtime took the country by storm.

Among other famous black ragtimers of the period were Louis Chauvin of St. Louis, Arthur Marshall and Scott Hayden, both of Sedalia, and James Scott of Neosho. Adding two ragtime compositions to the state's treasury of musical achievement was another famous black Missourian, J. W. "Blind" Boone of Columbia, a world-renowned composer and concert pianist. His Blind Boone Concert Company performed for forty-seven years across North America, winning black and white listeners everywhere.

Ragtime introduced black music into the heart of American musical culture, as the musical tradition born in slavery was shaped and honed to express new realities of the black existence. While many are familiar with the name Scott Joplin, the name James Scott is less well known. Scott was born in Neosho in 1886, the son of former slaves from North Carolina who had moved west. He was introduced into the world of music-making by his mother, who played by ear. An eager pupil, his unusual talent captured the attention of a local black musician named John Coleman early in his life. Coleman took the young musical genius on as a student and gave him formal musical training.

About the time Joplin's "Maple Leaf Rag" was gaining acceptance, James Scott, whose family had moved for a brief time to Ottawa, Kansas, composed his first piece on a reed pump organ. By the time Scott moved back to Carthage with his family in 1901, he was rapidly becoming an accomplished musician. At fifteen he could play difficult classical pieces and was beginning to find work as a pianist to add to his income from shining shoes.

Opportunity called when he took a job as janitor with Dumars Music Company in Carthage. In 1903, Dumars published Scott's "A Summer Breeze March and Two Step." By 1906, when James Scott met Scott Joplin, who was visiting Carthage, Dumars had published five of the young composer's rags. Shortly afterward, James Scott traveled to St. Louis to visit Joplin. That same year, Stark Music Company, Joplin's publisher, published James Scott's "Frog Legs." The stream of James Scott music that followed, and his reputation for artistic precision, earned him the title "Crown Prince of Ragtime." Although the ragtime era had waned, Scott continued with his rag compositions after he moved to Kansas City, Kansas, in 1920 and set up a teaching studio. He soon turned to work as a theater musician in Kansas City, where he died in 1930.

CHAPTER 5

Living with Jim Crow

U NTIL 1896, the white and black communities lived separately in Missouri, and black people were subjected to segregation and discrimination, but no federal law dictated this separation. In 1896, however, a landmark decision handed down by the U.S. Supreme Court in the case of *Plessy v. Ferguson* made segregation the law of the land. The court upheld a Louisiana law, which called for separate accommodations on trains for white and black passengers. That decision opened the door to complete segregation of black citizens, and "separate but equal" became the rule, if not the reality, in many states.

"Separate but equal" determined the status of blacks and whites in America for decades to come. Through two world wars and the Great Depression and until the desegregation of public schools in the 1950s, African Americans in Missouri, like their counterparts in other areas of the country, were for the most part restricted to their own communities. If not equal, they were in fact separate.

Many who had been emancipated without skills had seized upon the opportunity to acquire them in order to earn a living. Some, like William Kunze of Warren County, found benefactors to assist them. With the help of a German farmer, Kunze learned the trade of chairmaking and went on to enjoy a prosperous business as a result. His excellent craftsmanship, demonstrated in the careful attention to detail with which he fashioned his chairs, earned him a prominent name in chair design. Many examples of his products, both painted and unfinished, are still in existence, indicating to art historians that he had a thriving business.

As they had once been bound by slavery, the freed people were now bound by ties of color and condition. The tradition of community underwent its greatest test during this period. Using the tools of mutual aid and self-help, communities expanded customs and traditions to accommodate their separate but almost always less-than-equal status.

They used their skills as carpenters and stonemasons to build homes, churches, and businesses. They held "rent parties" to pay their rent. They took in laundry and scrubbed floors. They opened restaurants, blacksmith shops, barber shops, and shoeshine parlors. They educated themselves, each other, and their children.

Life under Jim Crow was hard to sustain even among the able-bodied. For the sick, it was often impossible. Nearly all communities had a practitioner of folk medicine or a midwife, who was called on when a member of the community was sick. The medicines prescribed usually consisted of herbs and other plants (sometimes the leaves and sometimes the roots). Older women usually treated the sick, primarily because of their age and experience with bedside nursing.

Blacks in towns and cities were often relegated to the most squalid areas, jammed together in shacks and shanties, generally without water or sewer services. The few white doctors that would treat their ailments usually did so after hours, when the presence of the patients of color would not be offensive to white patients.

Some blacks had been able to attend northern medical schools and practice medicine even before the Civil War. The first black medical school, at Howard University in Washington, D. C., opened in 1868. In 1896, Meharry Medical College was founded in Nashville, Tennessee; however, facilities at these schools were inadequate, and positions for black doctors were limited primarily to the Freedmen's Hospital in Washingon, D. C.

A HOSPITAL for COLORED PEOPLE

Headquarters: Masonic Temple, 18th and Woodland Avenue

The colored people of this city, assisted and advised by many prominent white people, will launch a campaign, beginningDecember 8 and continuing twenty days, to raise $25,000.00 to purchase and equip a permanent home for the Wheatley-Provident Hospital for colored people.

There Is No Hospital In This Great City That Admits Negro Physicians and Negro Patients Except THE OLD CITY HOSPITAL

Don't you think we deserve better treatment than that? BLACK MEN, LET US DO OUR DUTY. Remembering: "God helps those who HELP themselves." Many generous white people will help us.

Note: We have closed a deal for the Catholic school property at 1826 Forest avenue. It is a large, commodious stone building containing 20 large rooms IN THE HEART OF THE NEGRO DISTRICT, splendidly located and admirably suited for a Negro hospital.

It will require $25,000 to pay for and equip this property. Can't we get it? Bell Phone East **999**. Home Phone **Special.**

Mrs. T. G. McCampbell, President of Federated Clubs, will have charge of our annual Tag Day, Dec. 22.

The Wheatley-Provident Hospital

NELSON C. CREWS, Chairman Executive Committee
FRED W. DABNEY, Secretary Executive Committee

C. A. FRANKLIN, President
EVA M. FOX, Secretary

The black citizens of Kansas City needed a hospital and set out to get one. (State Historical Society of Missouri, Columbia, courtesy Missouri State Museum.)

When blacks were finally admitted as patients to hospitals in Missouri, they were generally confined to special wards or to the basement. In some areas, a separate house or building was set aside for them as a city hospital. The People's Hospital in St. Louis opened in 1894. It was the only facility in the city where black doctors could treat private patients, and it initiated nursing programs for black women in 1898. Renamed Provident Hospital in 1918, it served the community until 1978. A group of seventeen black physicians, under the leadership of black businessman Christopher Robinson, persuaded the city to open City Hospital No. 2 for blacks in 1918. That hospital also became a training facility for black physicians and nurses. It served the community until the Homer G. Phillips Hospital was dedicated in 1937.

The new facility, built at a cost of three million dollars, was named in honor of the black attorney and activist who had fought to include its funding in a 1923 bond issue. It offered internships certified by the American Medical Association in a variety of specialties as well as training in its School of Nursing. The Homer G. Phillips Hospital, which closed in 1979, was placed on the National Register of Historic Places in 1982.

In 1910, in Kansas City, John Edward Perry, a black physician, set up a fifteen-bed hospital for blacks. He also founded a training program for nurses at his Perry Sanitarium. The name was changed in 1915 to Provident Hospital and Nurse Training Association. A separate city hospital where black physicians and nurses could practice was established in the late 1920s. Still, in 1930, the death rate for black infants was twice that for white infants, and even into the 1950s four times more blacks than whites were dying from tuberculosis.

African Americans in Missouri struggled for access to health care from trained doctors and nurses. Depending once again on self-help and mutual aid, community members cooked and sold dinners to raise money to fund their institutions. They pooled their meager earnings to help the sick, the old, and the orphaned.

In spite of the barriers African Americans faced, Missouri's black communities produced doctors, lawyers, teachers, writers, comedians, opera singers, and scientists. The state's most outstanding black scientist was born in 1864 on a farm near Diamond in Newton County. His parents were slaves, and he was orphaned at an early age. From these humble beginnings, George Washington Carver grew up to become the agricultural scientist who is credited by many with revolutionizing southern agriculture.

Carver taught himself about plants through observation on the Carver farm and worked his way through school, beginning with Lincoln School in Neosho as an adolescent. Ultimately, he graduated from Simpson College and Iowa State Agricultural College at Ames. In 1896, the same year that the

George Washington Carver statue at George Washington Carver National Monument. (Photo by A. E. Schroeder)

U.S. Supreme Court decided *Plessy v. Ferguson,* Carver accepted the position of director of agricultural research at Tuskegee Institute in Alabama, a struggling black school founded by Booker T. Washington. There he had his own laboratory, as well as an experimental farm on the school grounds for the purpose of carrying out his research.

In 1914, the southern cotton industry was hit by a massive boll weevil attack, and Carver set out to develop alternative crops to reduce the South's dependence on cotton. In his experiments, he was able to develop over three hundred products from the peanut, including plastics, linoleum, wood filler, paper, ink, bleach, and synthetic rubber. He pioneered the process of extracting flour, breakfast food, and milk from soybeans and developed more than one hundred products from sweet potatoes. He produced five hundred shades of dye from plants native to the South and a talcum powder made of clay.

His discoveries enabled southern farmers to diversify their crops, and Carver also undertook to reeducate farmers in the Tuskegee area in ways to manage alternative crops. When George Washington Carver died in 1943, he had achieved distinction as one of America's finest scientists. He presented African Americans with a living example of how one could overcome great obstacles to achieve success. A national monument and a nature trail in Diamond, Missouri, honor this great scientist.

Although poor in material things, African Americans were rich in culture and tradition. With sacrifice, determination, and commitment, the black people of the United States used their traditions to shape their communities. Just as they worked together to build churches, schools, and self-help organizations, they developed a self-contained social life. Since African American men were not permitted to join white Masonic lodges, they formed their own lodges. They named their lodges in honor of Prince Hall, the founder of the first fraternal organization for blacks. Black men and women formed art and literature clubs and theater groups, such as the Morrison Players in Kansas City. The segregated community continued to express itself through music and dance.

Internationally acclaimed entertainer Josephine Baker of St. Louis came out of the dance tradition transported from Africa. Born into poverty, Baker claimed that she started dancing just to keep warm. She began as a child performing on sidewalks for pennies and went on to the New York stage in the 1920s. An ardent civil rights activist, Baker became a French citizen in 1937, exiling herself because of the discrimination she and other black entertainers faced in the United States. She earned great fame and success as an entertainer in France, where she came to be known as the "Black Venus." The French government decorated her with the "Medal of Resistance" for her work against the Nazi occupation during World War II. Josephine Baker visited the United States in 1951 but refused to perform before segregated audiences. She returned to France, retired from the stage, and raised twelve adopted children. Baker suffered two heart attacks in 1964, but she staged a triumphant comeback at New York's Carnegie Hall in 1973 and then suffered a third attack. She went on to open a new revue in Paris in 1975 but two days later was stricken by a cerebral hemorrhage and died. A public funeral was held for Josephine Baker in Paris. She received a twenty-one-gun salute, the only American woman to have been so honored.

During the twentieth century many black Americans achieved fame through music. By the 1920s black nightlife was flourishing. The blues, yet another descendant of the Negro spiritual, became the gospel of the streets and was popularized by the publication of "The St. Louis Blues," composed by musician W. C. Handy of Memphis, Tennessee. The song was based on his experiences during a two-week visit to St. Louis in 1893.

Josephine Baker, the toast of Paris. (Western Historical Manuscript Collection, St. Louis)

Broke, hungry, and unable to find a job, Handy slept in a vacant lot and underneath a bridge for shelter. He met the victim of another kind of misery walking along the levee. A woman was crying her heart out over problems she was having with her man. Handy, who was the leader of a small jazz ensemble, had previously written "Memphis Blues." Later, he used his memories of the woman at the levee as an inspiration, and "The St. Louis Blues" was born. The song reached the height of its popularity in a recording by noted blues singer Bessie Smith in 1925.

African American music also reigned on the other side of the state. From 1925 until the end of World War II, musicians often described life in Kansas City as "one long twenty-year jam session." Officials did not enforce Prohibition, and gambling and drinking in the heart of the community earned the city the reputation of being a wide-open town under political boss Tom Pendergast.

Jazz, which had traveled up the Mississippi from New Orleans by riverboat, inherited the ragtime throne in the kingdom of black music. Will "Count" Basie is credited with putting a Kansas City brand on it. The piano player and his band, the Kansas City Seven, were popular performers at the more than fifty white saloons and clubs that made up Kansas City's notorious nightlife. The Kansas City jazz scene included many of the great black musicians of that period, among them Charlie Parker and Joe Turner. The contribution of Missouri's African American musicians to the history of American music is truly one of the state's proudest traditions.

The art of storytelling, an honored part of the African oral tradition that had woven its way into the Negro spirituals, found a new means of expression with pen and paper. A great storyteller, the renowned poet Langston Hughes, born in Joplin in 1902, became one of America's most honored and productive authors. Hughes, whose college education included days at Columbia University and at Lincoln University in Pennsylvania, became known as the "Bard of African American Literature." He wrote volumes of poems, songs, novels, plays, biographies, histories, and essays: The University of Missouri Press edition of the complete "Collected Works of Langston Hughes" will come to eighteen volumes. Universal themes echo through his stories of ordinary black folks. His words speak of their joys and sorrows, their trials and tribulations, and their victories and defeats. As a New York critic wrote, "[Hughes] is one of the essential figures in American literature. . . . By his work and his example, he has enriched our lives."

Hughes emerged as an important man of letters during the Harlem Renaissance. In 1930, he began to earn his living as a writer. His volumes of verse include *The Weary Blues, Shakespeare in Harlem,* and *The Dream Keeper.* His novels are *Not without Laughter* and *Tambourines to Glory.* His autobiography, *The Big Sea,* was published in 1940. A world traveler, Hughes lived in many countries, including Haiti, Mexico, France, Italy, and Russia. He was both a Rosenwald and Guggenheim fellow and the recipient of many other awards and honors. Langston Hughes died in 1967.

Another form of storytelling, the folk ballad, gained prominence during the early twentieth century. Many ballads were born in St. Louis, including the "Ballad of Stackerlee" or "Stagolee." This ballad has many versions, some with as many as fifty stanzas, relating the numerous exploits attributed to the title character. Some folklorists believe the song relates the death of Billy Lyon in Memphis or elsewhere, but John R. David has found convincing evidence that the ballad tells the story of an incident that occurred in a St. Louis bar in the 1890s. According to one version of the ballad, a man named Billy Lyons removed his magic hat (which he had acquired in a pact with the devil) from the head of Lee Shelton, nicknamed Stack Lee, while he was sitting at the gambling table. In spite of Lyons's pleas, Stack Lee pulled out a gun and shot him to death. According to David, Stacker Lee

Langston Hughes.
(Library of Congress)

went to the Missouri State Penitentiary for the crime.

None of the ballads, however, became more popular than the one about "Frankie and Johnnie," which historians believe originated in a St. Louis boardinghouse and relates the story of Frankie Baker's murder of her young, two-timing boyfriend Allen, or Albert, Britt.

> Frankie and Johnnie were lovers,
> Oh Lordy how they could love,
> They swore to be true to each other
> Just as true as the stars above,
> He was her man, but he done her wrong.

On Sunday, October 15, 1899, in a room in a boardinghouse on Targee Street in St. Louis, Frankie shot her lover dead. According to Frankie Baker, the "Ballad of Frankie and Johnnie" is based on that event, although some people claim they heard the ballad many years before Frankie shot her boyfriend. In any case, the song captured the public's imagination, and before long singers were including it in their repertoires, and bartenders were creating drinks based on the legend. Screen star Mae West memorialized it by using it in her play *Diamond Lil* and in the movie *She Done Him Wrong*.

Frankie Baker was born in St. Louis on May 30, 1876. As a teenager, she fell in love with a waiter. His girlfriend broke into the Baker home and slashed Frankie across the face, causing a wound that required thirty-eight stitches to close. Frankie claimed the incident led her to become a part of the fast life in St. Louis's bars. Albert Britt was born in Kentucky in 1882 and moved to St. Louis with his parents in 1891. He grew into a handsome young man and became a piano player. He and Frankie met and became lovers.

Frankie claimed that she spent her earnings dressing Albert in the finest clothes. Apparently, other women were also attracted to him, and Albert returned their attentions. Frankie was living with her younger brother and a girlfriend in the house on Targee Street at the time of the murder. She said she heard that Albert had taken up with a woman named Alice Pryor, and when he came into her room in the middle of the night, he had been drinking and threatened her. As he pulled a knife from his pocket and started toward her, Frankie said, she grabbed the gun she kept under her pillow and shot him. The coroner's jury accepted her story and ruled the killing a justifiable homicide committed in self-defense.

Some contend that the song "Frankie and Al" became popular a few months after the murder, but young Britt's father created such a furor over it that the name of the ballad, which many said was composed by a black pianist named Bill Dooley, was changed to "Frankie and Johnnie." Although she had been acquitted of murder, the event haunted Frankie, and she left St. Louis a year later, moving first to Omaha and then, in 1915, to Portland, Oregon. A brief stint in the sporting life earned her some time in jail. When she became ill and could no longer work, she filed suit against Mae West and Paramount Pictures over the use of her name, but the case never went to trial. The press became interested, and Frankie went public with her story. She filed another suit in 1938 against Republic Pictures, claiming that her reputation had been damaged in that company's production of "Frankie and Johnny."

She lost the suit, her health continued to decline, and by 1949 she was on public relief. She was ultimately declared mentally ill and placed in the East Oregon Hospital, where she died in 1952. The "Ballad of Frankie and Johnnie" lives on. In his *American Songbag,* poet Carl Sandburg wrote that "The Frankie songs at best are American parallels of certain European ballads of low life that are rendered by important musical artists from the continent for enthusiastic audiences in Carnegie Hall in New York or Orchestra Hall in Chicago." He predicted that "as American culture advances, it may be that classes will take up the Frankie songs as seriously as . . . the Provencal ballads of France." This has been the case with the song Frankie Baker said told her story.

Frankie's era was one in which personal style was as important to African Americans as it is today. This was the age of conked hair, zoot suits, boogie-woogie, and the jitterbug. Still facing discrimination by whites because of their skin color and hair texture, some blacks continued to experiment with formulas to lighten skin and straighten hair. Such ingredients as potatoes, potash, lye, and hot fat were sometimes mixed together for use as hair straighteners. Charcoal, kerosene, and even cornmeal were employed to clean the hair. Coffee was often used as a dye. Women applied egg facials to condition and tighten their skin and enhance their complexions.

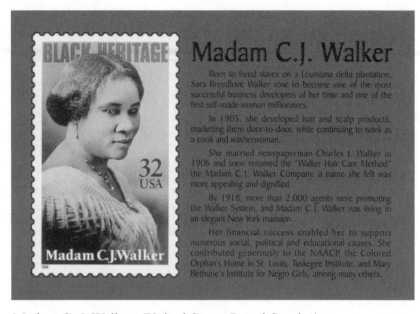

Madam C. J. Walker. (United States Postal Service)

Two African American women pioneered in the field of hair and skin care in the early 1900s. Sarah McWilliams Walker, known as Madam C. J. Walker, developed a hair-straightening method and manufactured a complete line of hair preparations, toilet articles, and cosmetics, which she sold door to door. Although she launched her career in Indianapolis, Indiana, her early experiments took place in St. Louis in the 1890s when she was working as a laundress. Walker employed agents and operated beauty schools throughout the United States, including one in Kansas City.

Annie Turnbo Malone, of Metropolis, Illinois, established Poro College and School of Beauty Culture in St. Louis around 1904. Malone, a philanthropist and community activist, was instrumental in developing a permanent straightening treatment for kinky hair. In addition to operating the school, Malone started a distributing company and helped many of her graduates in careers as Poro agents or operators of their own salons.

Baseball was a popular neighborhood sport in black communities in the first half of the twentieth century. Neighborhoods and towns had their own teams and competed with one another throughout the summer. Black professional baseball made its Missouri debut with the St. Louis Giants around 1914. The team changed its name in 1922 to the St. Louis Stars. Its most famous player was Mississippi native James "Cool Papa" Bell, whose baseball career began at age sixteen. Bell was a center fielder who played professionally in the Negro National League from 1922 to 1950.

The Kansas City Monarchs came on the Negro National League scene in 1919 and soon practically dominated it, winning championships in 1923, 1924, and 1929. In 1924, the team also won the first Negro World Series when it beat a team from Pennsylvania belonging to the Eastern Colored League. Between 1938 and 1946 the Monarchs earned another five pennants. By that time their most famous player, Satchel Paige, was a member of the team.

Leroy "Satchel" Paige was probably born on July 7, 1906. Even his mother claimed not to know for sure. He was the seventh of eleven children born to John and Lula Paige. His father was a gardener and his mother a washwoman. As a child, he was a sometime student who also worked to help supplement his family's small income. He earned the nickname "Satchel" by putting a pole and some ropes together to carry several suitcases at once when he went to work as a baggage boy at the train station in Mobile, Alabama.

His hobby was throwing rocks; he and his friends would practice their aim, using the rocks to knock over empty cans. His baseball career began at the age of ten with his school team. He played first base and outfield. When the team's two pitchers gave up six runs in the first inning of a midseason game, the coach decided to give Satchel a try at the mound. His first time up, he struck out sixteen batters, not giving up a single hit. Following that performance he became the team's main pitcher.

Paige's career took a curious twist two years later, when he was caught shoplifting a toy wand. He was sent to the Industrial School for Negro Boys at Mt. Meigs, Alabama, where he stayed for more than five years. Fortunately, the reform school had a baseball team and a coach who helped the boy mold his talent. With the coach's help and lots of practice, Satchel learned to control his pitching.

He left reform school in 1923, at the age of seventeen. By that time he was six feet, three inches tall. He tried out with his brother's semi-pro baseball team, the Mobile Tigers, and when the coach was unable to hit any of the ten balls Paige threw, he hired the teenager. His fancy pitching quickly made him a folk hero. He joined the Chattanooga Black Lookouts in 1926 and the following year went to the Birmingham Black Barons. After playing winter ball in the West Indies and Latin America, he joined the Elite Giants in Nashville and Cleveland. A stint with the Pittsburgh Crawfords allowed him to try his style out against white teams. During a stormy career with the Crawfords, he was banned from Negro baseball for walking out on his contract, but the ban was lifted, and he rejoined the team. At the height of his career, he suffered an injury to his shoulder in Mexico City and was told he would never pitch again.

After that several coaches turned him down; then the owner of the Kansas City Monarchs invited him to play on his traveling team. With the help of his coach he began to get his pitching arm back in shape. After months of struggle, he regained the use of his pitching arm. He joined the Monarchs A team and became their ace pitcher. In August 1971, eleven years before his death in 1982, Leroy "Satchel" Paige was officially inducted into the Baseball Hall of Fame.

Jackie Robinson, who broke the color line in professional baseball by joining the Brooklyn Dodgers in 1947, began playing with the Monarchs in 1946. In their heyday, the Monarchs drew as many as fifteen thousand hometown fans, and often as many as nineteen thousand attended their Sunday games. They were the first professional team to play night games.

Ironically, Jackie Robinson's magnificent showing while playing for the Monarchs led to the demise of black professional baseball teams. Once white professional baseball opened its ranks to African Americans, the old black teams began to lose their fans, although the St. Louis Cardinals' lineup was not integrated until 1954. Tom Alston was the first black player signed by the Cardinals. The proud legacy of black professional baseball is one more landmark in the history of Missouri sports.

The dire poverty and oppression suffered by the majority of people in the segregated urban communities made them easy prey for con artists. The indifference of some government officials to such matters as health care and legal protection for black Americans left communities open to the ravages of disease, alcohol, drug abuse, and con games. Empty promises to relieve their burdens were always at hand.

Crap games, numbers parlors, and policy wheels, much like the lotteries of today and promising "quick riches," became important institutions in African American communities. Children often went door to door selling punchboard numbers, offering people the opportunity to purchase a chance for a coveted prize. Commercially printed "Dream Books" were common household articles. These books claimed to interpret dreams and convert them to numbers that the dreamer should play to win money.

If one dreamed of apples, for instance, the dream book would say that seeing apples in your sleep meant joy and happiness, and ripe apples were the sign of health and wealth. In that case, advised the dream book, one should play the numbers 9-4-0. The dream book recommended that all numbers be played for three days to ensure success. It was the job of "runners" to pick up the numbers from house to house, and winners were drawn daily. The winners got such small amounts that they usually gambled their winnings in the hope of getting more.

Also hoping to change their luck were the many people especially vulnerable to practitioners of "black magic." They called it making "gris-gris." For those who were seeking power or greater prosperity, there was a magic that, like jazz, had traveled up the Mississippi from New Orleans. It was known as voodoo. Historians believe this strange religion originated in Dahomey, today's Nigeria, in West Africa, where Africans were captured by raiders seeking slaves for the New World. Those captured, brought by the French from Haiti to Louisiana in the eighteenth century, introduced voodoo to the United States. Although Vodo was the name of the god they served, the word was corrupted to voodoo, voudou, or similar names, which have been used for both the sect and its rites and practices. "Gris-gris" is the word used for the alleged magic-making and various charms and spells.

Before the religion arrived in Missouri, a succession of voodoo queens and kings held court in New Orleans. The city's most famous practitioner was Marie Laveau, a free mulatto, who was born about 1796 and dominated voodooism for about forty years. Voodoo doctors are usually people who learned the practice through oral tradition and demonstration when they were children. Magic powers are sometimes believed to be a gift to people who have a physical distinction.

A black man named Alexander was reportedly the "King of the Voodoos" in the Missouri Valley in the early 1900s. As such, he was to train a number of priests and priestesses in the art. According to the voodoo king's explanation to Mary Alicia

Owen of St. Joseph, the trained conjurer needs no tricks, but he must have a strong will. To become a practitioner of the art required rigorous training. Alexander's trainees were expected to undergo fasting, sleeplessness, and cold. They were required to burn, cut, bruise, and lash themselves and feel no suffering. They were made to drink strange mixtures, swallow tobacco smoke, walk in cemeteries, and dance until their feet bled and their minds were confused. It took months or years before the trainee achieved a high rank. The voodoo motto was "Control yourself perfectly, and you can control the world—organic and inorganic," according to Owen.

While voodoo was probably most often practiced in the cities, where more lucrative opportunities existed, a man called Guinea Sam living in Boonville in mid-Missouri was a well-known practitioner. Guinea, whose real name was Sam Nightingale, arrived in Boonville in 1856, brought to the town by Horatio Ellis, a doctor from Louisiana. Guinea Sam claimed to be a native African and said his nickname came from the fact that he was born on what was known as the Guinea Coast of Africa. He spoke with a strange accent.

His reputation was well known in Boonville, where he doctored with herbal medicine, created love potions, cast magic spells, worked charms, and played tricks. Guinea Sam worked the Boonville area for some thirty years. Although some people said he disappeared in a cloud of blue smoke, his obituary appeared in a Boonville newspaper on August 5, 1887, listing the date of his death as August 4. Contemporaries estimated him to be nearly one hundred years old.

Voodoo practitioners and conjurers held a respected place in the segregated black communities of Missouri. Although feared by many, they were credited with great powers and said to have charms and magic potions for all purposes. They could place curses on someone's enemies, bring back wayward wives and husbands, cause good or bad luck, and drive people crazy or cure whatever ailed them. To be sure, voodoo had its greatest appeal among the poor and uneducated. Those who lived under the burden of oppression were likely to turn to any source that promised relief.

Slavery had taught African Americans the importance of communication in preserving their communities. Information had passed by word of mouth, sometimes in song, sometimes in whispers. Following Emancipation, communication was vital in maintaining the communities' determination to achieve equality and justice. Keeping issues of importance uppermost in the minds of the people was a major priority in the fight for first-class citizenship.

Church leaders took on the task of writing and distributing information for their members and the community at large. "The Book of Concern of the African Methodist Episcopal Church," headquartered in Philadelphia, Pennsylvania, had organized in 1855 and soon began to publish the *Christian Herald* and other literature for its churches, including those in Missouri.

The *St. Louis Negro World* began publishing in 1875, and the *Freedman's Record* appeared in Kansas City as early as 1876. Sixteen black newspapers were operating in Missouri by the 1890s, including the *Jefferson City Western Messenger,* the *Macon Messenger,* and the *Sedalia Times.* These early publications had a common theme: They all sought to encourage cooperative black enterprise.

By 1897, George R. Smith College in Sedalia had added a print department to its facilities and in May of that year began publishing a school newspaper, the *Kinetoscope,* which was later renamed the *Smithsonian.* It also established a journal, the *Weekly Conservator,* which dealt with racial issues, promoted the advancement of blacks, and discussed new methods of education. It ultimately became known as one of the best publications in Missouri.

In Columbia, Rufus Logan published the city's first black

newspaper in 1901. It was called the *Professional World* and remained in publication until 1902. Logan argued for the establishment of black businesses in the community and for a black hospital.

The *St. Louis Argus* was established by brothers Joseph and William Mitchell and William's wife, Nannie Mitchell, around 1912. It became a leading voice in advocating civil rights for African Americans. Chester Franklin, an experienced journalist, founded the *Kansas City Call* in 1919. He had assisted his father, George, in publishing a weekly called the *Omaha Enterprise* in Nebraska and later a paper in Denver called the *Star* before coming to Kansas City.

A famous African American who worked for the *Call* was Roy Wilkins, who later became executive director of the NAACP. Franklin hired Wilkins in 1923. Before he left the paper nearly ten years later, he was writing a popular weekly column and serving as its news editor. Lucille Bluford succeeded Franklin as editor and publisher of the weekly *Call* in 1955. In 1939, Bluford had sued the University of Missouri in an attempt to gain admission to its school of journalism. The university and the state refused to admit her; instead, Missouri created a school of journalism at Lincoln University.

The black press in Missouri has played a valuable role in the progress toward equal justice and has helped ensure the continuity of the African American culture since the days following Emancipation. It is an important tradition and one that is highly honored by African Americans.

For over one hundred years—from the mid-1860s until the late 1960s—African Americans in Missouri concentrated most of their efforts on building and sustaining communities, but they continued to protest the limitations of their segregated lifestyle. Meanwhile, black businesses flourished, religious life blossomed, and cultural life was rich and colorful.

They made their own music and entertained themselves.

They passed on to their children the customs and traditions that had made their survival possible. They taught them to sing, dance, tell stories, and amuse themselves with games and rhymes:

> Hambone, hambone / Where've you been?
> Around the world / And back again.
> Hambone, hambone / Where's your wife?
> In the kitchen / Sharpening her knife.
> Hambone, hambone / Where'd you stay?
> I met a girl / And ran away.

Still, discrimination and, often, danger pervaded every area of African American life during this era. From the end of the Civil War through the early decades of the twentieth century, some whites carried out a reign of terror against the black people of the state. In 1924, the Ku Klux Klan was at the height of its popularity in Missouri. While the Klan's membership tended to be more rural than urban, St. Joseph provided a forum for pro-Klan propaganda through a weekly newspaper, *Missouri Valley Independent,* published there.

The Klan and other segregationists opposed all the advances that black people sought. Equal access to education and health services, the right to hold a decent job and to purchase a home in the neighborhood of one's choice, the right to use public facilities—all these had to be achieved by means of protests and lawsuits. The Missouri Equal Rights League, the first state political activist organization in the United States, had been formed in 1865 in St. Louis. This group was responsible for leading the fight to gain the right to vote for black men and the right of access to public education for black children. When the right to vote for black men was granted in 1870, with the adoption of the Fifteenth Amendment to the U.S. Constitution, the Equal Rights League had massed its strength behind the school movement.

Shortly after the turn of the century, state chapters of the NAACP and the National Urban League assumed the tasks of promoting better job opportunities, providing social and legal services for blacks, and working for equal rights. These rights were not easily won, as the Lloyd Gaines case demonstrated. Gaines's disappearance in 1939 remains one of the most compelling mysteries in the history of the struggle for equal rights in Missouri. A Mississippi native, Lloyd Gaines came to St. Louis with his family as a fourteen-year-old and graduated first in his class at Vashon High School in 1926. He won a $250 scholarship in an essay contest and enrolled as a freshman at Stowe Teachers College. The following year, he transferred to Lincoln University and graduated with honors in 1935 as president of his class.

Gaines wanted to be a lawyer, but state laws prohibited the University of Missouri from admitting black students. In *Making Civil Rights Law,* Mark V. Tushnet writes that the "NAACP's first Supreme Court victory in the coordinated attack on segregation" occurred in the Gaines case in 1938. When Gaines applied to the University of Missouri, officials there advised him to apply to Lincoln, which had no law school, saying Lincoln would establish a law school if he applied. This was clearly unsatisfactory since a newly opened school could not be "equal." Gaines and the NAACP decided to challenge the "separate but equal" doctrine. With the assistance of Sidney R. Redman, the leading African American attorney in St. Louis, Gaines filed suit in state court against the University of Missouri for rejecting his application for admittance to the law school. The court found in favor of the state's segregation laws, "to no one's surprise." When the case was appealed to the Missouri Supreme Court, that court ruled that because the state provided scholarship assistance for black students to attend out-of-state graduate schools, its actions did not violate the equal protection clause of the Constitution; therefore, the state had complied with the Fourteenth Amendment.

Newspaper headlines from the time of Lloyd Gaines's disappearance. (MU Publications and Alumni Communication)

Gaines's attorneys then appealed to the United States Supreme Court. While this action was pending, Gaines enrolled in graduate school at the University of Michigan. He received a master's degree in economics in 1937. In 1938, the U.S. Supreme Court ruled against the state. Its decision held that Missouri had an obligation to provide equal educational opportunities within its borders and gave the state three options: admit Gaines to the University of Missouri, close its law school, or create a separate but equal law school for black students.

Following the Supreme Court ruling Gaines returned to St. Louis and announced his decision to enter the university. However, the Missouri legislature, seeking to avert this, passed a law providing Lincoln University with $275,000 to establish its own law school. This new law school opened in the Poro College building in St. Louis with an enrollment of thirty students. Lloyd Gaines, however, was not among them. On April 27, 1939, he left for Chicago, after telling an acquaintance that he planned to spend a few days there and then return to St. Louis. He was last seen leaving a fraternity house in Chicago where he was staying. There is no evidence he ever returned to St. Louis. Although numerous attempts were made to locate him, and his photograph was published in newspapers across the nation, Lloyd Gaines was never heard from again. While Gaines's success in earning the right to equal education under the laws of Missouri did not overturn the "separate but equal" doctrine, according to Tushnet it was "the first substantial inroad" toward that end. Eventually the efforts to obtain equal opportunity led to school desegregation throughout the country.

Also in 1939, the year that Lloyd Gaines had hoped to win a victory for black education over the forces of segregation, black and white sharecroppers, evicted from farms in southeast Missouri, spread out along the highway near Sikeston to protest the low pay and harsh living conditions inflicted on them by the practices of some white planters. This spectacular outpouring of farmers into the public's view along Missouri highways is most often referred to as the Sharecroppers Roadside Demonstration of 1939. The leader of the protest was a remarkable man.

Owen Whitfield was one of the many farmers who had migrated from the South in the 1920s to the fertile areas of southeast Missouri. Although he had attended college in Mississippi, it was, by his own assessment, an unsatisfactory educational experience. In his new location, he took up the work he knew best, farming, taking advantage of the only financial opportunity open to a man of his race and skills, sharecropping. He also became a preacher, and by the mid-1930s, he was serving as pastor for several black churches in the area.

Concern for the plight of farm workers had led to the organization of the Southern Tenant Farmers Union (STFU) in Arkansas in 1934 to address the problems of sharecroppers in the South. In 1937 Whitfield joined the organization, and his vigorous preaching style quickly gained the attention of the union's leadership. He soon became one of its most influential members. Since the union was predominantly a white organization, the election of Whitfield as second vice president in 1938 helped the group attract black farmers to their cause.

The life of sharecroppers in southeast Missouri in the 1930s was one of hardship and poverty. Matters got even worse when federal legislation made it more profitable for farmers to replace sharecroppers with day laborers: Sharecroppers were entitled to a portion of the government payments to cotton farmers, and day laborers were not. Furthermore, the farmers used their payments to purchase tractors and other mechanized equipment so they would need fewer workers. Whitfield wasted no time in trying to get these issues before the proper authorities. In January of 1938 he wrote to President Franklin Roosevelt, pleading for his help in protecting the ten thousand suffering families who were under threat of eviction. For his efforts, Whitfield received a noncommittal reply from an employee of the Farm Security Administration.

Desperate to demonstrate the plight of his fellow cotton laborers, Whitfield decided to take desperate measures and planned a mass highway demonstration. On January 9, 1939, approximately eleven hundred sharecroppers, the majority of them black, camped out on the rights-of-way of U.S Highways 60 and 61 in southeastern Missouri. The camps stretched out across thirty-eight miles of Highway 60, east and west, and seventy miles of Highway 61, north and south, to criss-cross Sikeston. Although Whitfield, knowing his life could be in jeopardy, had gone to St. Louis, the demonstration captured the attention of the press and became front-page news. In less than a week, the state government, claiming that the highway camps constituted a threat to the public health, began moving the demonstrators, either back to their homes or into special camps away from the highways.

Roadside strike in Southeast Missouri. (Western Historical Manuscript Collection, St. Louis)

However, state officials eventually met with Whitfield and large landowners, and landowners agreed not to evict the tenants. In February of 1940 Whitfield quit the STFU and joined ranks with the United Cannery, Agricultural, Packing and Allied Workers of America, a union affiliated with the Congress of Industrial Organizations (CIO); he felt the former had given the demonstrators more assistance than the STFU had been able to do. And over the next two years, the Farm

Security Administration set up loan-grant programs for share-croppers and laborers, built group labor camps, and created several cooperatives for some of the workers. As a result of Whitfield's efforts, the lot of tenant farmers had been some-what improved. He left the union behind and moved on. When he died in 1965, he was the pastor of Pilgrims Rest Baptist Church in Mounds, Illinois. His strategy of protest, however, the roadside demonstration, formed a model for the protest marches of the civil rights movement.

Most of the changes that came about in Missouri in the century following Emancipation were due to the demands of civil rights groups, such as the Congress of Racial Equality (CORE) in St. Louis and lesser known but equally successful groups in other towns and cities across the state. Threatened lawsuits finally opened public swimming pools to blacks in Kansas City and St. Louis in the early 1950s. Sit-ins and boy-cotts characterized the years of protest in the mid-twentieth century.

Even such significant court cases as *Brown v. Board of Education of Topeka* of 1954, which led to the desegregation of the public schools, and legislation such as the Civil Rights Act of 1964 and the Voting Rights Act of 1965 did not move the state of Missouri to proceed with "all deliberate speed" to remove the obstacles that blocked black progress. So, protests continued, and the protestors became more militant. When Kansas City officials refused to close schools for the funeral of Martin Luther King, Jr., a riot broke out in which several civilians were killed and hundreds wounded. The Kansas City police had to call in the National Guard and the state police to bring the rioting under control.

But the traditions of community—self-help, mutual aid, cel-ebration, worship, song, entrepreneurship, style, and protest—born in the slave experience, survived the long night of Jim Crow. Customs and traditions were reinvented and reshaped by African Americans to celebrate the advances and accommodate the setbacks in their efforts to move forward. Their struggle to enjoy the full rights of citizenship in the state that their ancestors had labored to help develop was neither brief nor bloodless.

CHAPTER 6

The Slow Death of Jim Crow

T HE struggles of the last half of the twentieth century forever changed the face of the African American community. From the desegregation of the public schools to the
urban renewal projects of the 1950s, barrier after barrier fell,
and African Americans gradually began to experience new
freedoms.

With the new freedoms came new challenges. The tradition
of community, now centuries old, was swept away by the
winds of progress. In most small towns and cities, schools in
black neighborhoods were either closed or turned into special
education facilities or administrative offices. School buses
rolled through African American neighborhoods across much
of the state, and children eagerly climbed on board, anxious
to explore the new places, and opportunities, that were now,
supposedly, open to them.

Most black parents welcomed the chance to have their
children integrated into white schools with better facilities
than most black schools, up-to-date textbooks, and state-of-
the-art equipment. Parents had longed for better education
and more opportunities for their children, but the early days
of integration were not easy for the children. Some have
painful memories of white teachers and students who were
either hostile or simply did not recognize their presence.
Desegregation efforts were particularly difficult in Kansas
City and St. Louis, where large black communities were confined to all-black neighborhoods that constituted all-black
school districts. Consequently, desegregation plans of the

School bus and children in Mexico, Missouri. (Collection of Charles Fry)

state's two largest cities resulted in battles fought in the courts over decades.

   In the early days of desegregation, the opportunities seemed to far outweigh the losses of black teachers, many of whom saw their jobs disappear with desegregation, and the loss of the school buildings, which had been central meeting places in the communities. Residents anxiously watched the changes occurring as their children rode school buses out of the neighborhoods. Not only were their schools no longer available to them, but following the Federal Housing Act of 1949, the federal government joined forces with states, towns, and cities to deal with the issue of slum housing. Cities and towns formed development and housing authorities and made their own land clearance policies. These efforts resulted in massive buyouts of land, much of which was owned by blacks. The old neigh-

borhoods, home to many families since the days of emancipation, were ripped up; substandard housing was torn down and
replaced by rows of new apartment buildings. In many areas
of the state, neighborhoods that had been lined with dilapidated houses on rutted roads suddenly boasted smart-looking
apartments along paved streets. Sewers were dug, and rainwa-
ter, which had once formed puddles and whirlpools in the
thoroughfares, now swiftly drained away.

One of the earliest and largest of these rebuilding jobs, the
Pruitt-Igoe Housing Project in St. Louis, was completed during the mid-1950s. The two apartment buildings cost about
thirty-six million dollars. The complex comprised thirty-three
eleven-story buildings, and although the Igoe apartments were
built for white tenants, nearly all of the 11,500 tenants eventually housed in the buildings were black. At the time of its con-
struction, the Pruitt-Igoe complex was considered to have the
largest, best-designed units of the postwar era. By the early
1960s, most towns and cities had completed similar projects.

Such projects were often cosmetic changes designed to cor-
rect or simply cover evidence of past abuses, and the flaws
became apparent almost immediately. Large housing com-
plexes offered inadequate recreational spaces for the thousands of children in the units. They were often located too far
away from shopping facilities and health services, and in
many cases adequate public transportation was unavailable.
By the late 1960s, the neighborhood around the gigantic
Wayne Miner housing complex in Kansas City had become so
crime ridden that a private security company was employed to
guard the residents and the facility. Vandalism was rampant.
Halls stank from urine and feces; plumbing was ripped out;
and elevators were frequently inoperable. Whatever the answer
was to congested neighborhoods and substandard housing, it
became clear early on that high-rise public housing was not it.
The experiment failed and left many of the poor and indigent
worse off than before.

African Americans were still not free to purchase homes in the neighborhoods of their choice. One St. Louis couple, J. D. and Ethel Shelley, learned this lesson the hard way. After moving into a home they purchased in 1945, they found themselves defendants in a lawsuit filed by their neighbors, Louis and Fern Kraemer, who sought to evict them on the basis of a restrictive covenant attached to the house's deed. This restriction dated back to 1911 and barred the original or subsequent owners of the property from selling or leasing it to people who were not Caucasians.

The case represented a deliberate challenge to the legality of restrictive covenants, launched by black realtor James T. Bush, Sr., and an organization he formed in 1946 called the Real Estate Brokers Association. Bush had arranged for a white woman to purchase the home and resell it to the Shelleys. A three-year court battle ensued. The St. Louis Circuit Court refused to enforce the covenant and evict the Shelleys, but the Missouri Supreme Court reversed the lower court ruling. The Shelleys won their appeal to the U.S. Supreme Court, which handed down its decision on May 3, 1948, finding that restrictive covenants were in violation of the equal protection clause of the Fourteenth Amendment. Restrictive covenants in nineteen other states and Washington, D. C., were struck down by this ruling. Missouri, however, did not pass its Fair Housing Act until 1972.

In the meantime, other small barriers had fallen. In 1965, the state had passed its Public Accommodations Act, which gave African Americans access to all places that accommodated the public, such as hotels, restaurants, soda fountains, and ice cream parlors. Although Missouri had also passed the Fair Employment Practices Act in 1961, many blacks still had difficulty finding work.

African Americans in Missouri had joined others throughout America in applauding the Civil Rights Act of 1964, which removed most of the legal barriers that prevented them from

CORE marchers in Columbia in 1960. (Western Historical Manuscript Collection, Columbia)

obtaining first-class citizenship. With the doors finally opened, the people were restless and in no mood to brook the delays that often ensued. Protests and riots erupted throughout the country. In 1968, the assassination of Martin Luther King, Jr., in Memphis, Tennessee, caused racial tensions across the country to explode. With the exception of the racial conflict that developed in Kansas City, however, most of Missouri was spared open confrontation as black people continued to push quietly to take advantage of their new opportunities.

Many white people were uneasy with the rapid progress African Americans were making in the area of civil rights. Wearied by racial conflict, agitation for change, and the divisiveness of the Vietnam War, voters elected the conservative Richard Nixon as president of the United States in hope of a return to normalcy. The Nixon administration closed down fifty-nine Job Corps centers that had assisted blacks in finding employment and set about dismantling the programs that, under the Office of Economic Opportunity, had been designed by previous administrations to help African Americans and poor people merge into the mainstream of American life. A people who now called themselves blacks began to reassess their gains and reflect on their losses.

They became increasingly aware that their customs and traditions were slipping away. They saw their children grow into adults who had lost touch with their history and culture. African American history was not a subject that received much attention in schools. The traditional communities had become divided on the basis of economics. Many of the better educated, upwardly mobile African Americans had left the traditionally black communities for upscale housing in other neighborhoods. Schools, which had brought unity to the communities, had become dilapidated eyesores or had been demolished.

In the tradition of their ancestors, communities turned again to the one institution that had remained constant throughout their history—the church. Although the Catholic Church had

Log Providence Church is in the Three Creeks area of Boone County, which was settled by slaveholding families from the East. After the Civil War some black families remained and established farms. The church, once the center of community life, is now restored and draws former residents back for special events. The Missouri Conservation Department has established Three Creeks State Forest in the area. (State Historical Society of Missouri, Columbia)

maintained a certain openness to black members during the French and Spanish colonial periods, that did not continue when the Upper Louisiana territory opened to immigration after the Louisiana Purchase, leading to an influx of southern whites. Their racial attitudes prevailed in the Church, and separate parishes and schools were established for black people. It was not until the late 1940s that barriers of discrimination in Catholic schools and parishes began to fall in St. Louis. Since the 1950s, major Protestant congregations have also become multiracial.

Still, most African Americans continued to worship in their own churches and according to their own traditions. Baptist, Methodist, African Methodist, Christian Methodist, Christian Disciples', Pentecostal, and Holiness churches serve African American communities across Missouri. Traditional hymns, black gospel, historical and contemporary, and the Negro spiritual all still play a vital role in worship services. Choirs, choruses, quartets, and individual musicians carry on the traditional music from generation to generation. In many African American churches, worship continues as an emotionally charged experience, invigorated with soulful personal testimonies and prayers. Tent revivals remain a part of the summer with traveling evangelists calling sinners to repent, and church-related activities remain a large part of African American religious life. Weekly prayer meetings, choir rehearsals, church anniversaries, special programs, and fellowship dinners usually fill the church calendars, drawing members together.

As in the early tradition of the black church, many churches continue to operate as social institutions for the community. They provide outreach programs for the poor, daycare facilities, soup kitchens, and thrift shops. They offer meeting rooms for community groups and activity rooms for community children.

The 1950s saw the emergence of a new religious movement among African Americans as members of the Nation of Islam began to practice their faith in Missouri. The group, followers of Elijah Muhammad, established a mission in St. Louis and a mosque in Kansas City and carried their message around Missouri by offering their newspaper, *Muhammad Speaks,* for sale in communities throughout the state. The Islamic Center of Central Missouri, in Columbia, offers classes in language and religion and welcomes interested visitors to tour their facilities.

CHAPTER 7

A Charge to Keep

I N the 1980s and the 1990s African Americans made un-
paralleled political, social, and economic progress in Missouri. Kansas City elected its first black mayor, Emmanuel
Cleaver, in 1991, and St. Louis elected black mayor Freeman
Bosley in 1993. Following the lead of Walthall Moore, the first
African American elected to serve in the Missouri General
Assembly, in 1921, and William Clay, Sr., Missouri's first U.S.
Representative, in 1969, African Americans distinguished
themselves in ever greater numbers by winning seats in the
general assembly. Others began to serve on local school
boards and in local governments across the state.

A manager of one of Clay's early campaigns was Gwen
Giles, who, in 1977, became the first African American
woman elected to the Missouri State Senate after filling the
unexpired term of a senator from the fourth district.

During the civil rights movement of the 1960s, according
to biographer Betty Cook Rottmann, Giles had promoted the
involvement of St. Louis religious leaders in civil rights. She
was a member of the St. Louis Conference on Religion and
Race, the Archdiocesan Commission on Human Rights, and
the Black Catholic Association of the Archdiocese. In 1970,
Mayor A. J. Cervantes appointed Giles executive secretary of
the St. Louis Council on Human Relations, and in 1973, Mayor
John Poelker appointed her commissioner of human relations.
In that position she updated the city ordinance to protect
women, the elderly, and the disabled and worked for the passage of the 1976 Comprehensive Civil Rights Ordinance.

Gwen Giles. (State
Historical Society of
Missouri, Columbia)

As a Missouri state senator, Gwen Giles served on several
committees and sponsored bills for the ratification of the
Equal Rights Amendment, for direct bank deposits of public
assistance payments, for a change in the blue law to allow
shopping on Sundays, for compensation for personal injury
suffered by crime victims, and for aid to dependent children
of unemployed parents. She cochaired the legislative black
caucus and was twice a delegate to the National Democratic
Convention. President Jimmy Carter appointed her to serve
on a task force that assisted in selecting talented women for
positions in federal government.

Giles later became the first African American to be St. Louis assessor, a position she held until her death on March 15, 1986. Harris-Stowe State College of St. Louis has established a scholarship fund in her name, and Catalpa Park in St. Louis's West End and Wellston Post Office have been renamed in her honor.

In the private sector, as professionals and entrepreneurs, African Americans achieved status in nearly all fields of endeavor. Blacks were living in many neighborhoods that had formerly been closed to them, and great numbers had entered mainstream society.

Still, lack of education and job opportunities kept many members of black communities at or below the poverty level. Those problems plus violence and drug use, which had been well hidden behind the shroud of segregation, and pregnancies of unwed teenagers plagued communities. At the same time, with families scattered, neighbors dislocated, and schools closed down, the sense of community that had sustained blacks through the troubles of the past was lost. That loss was deeply felt and openly mourned. Many people felt the need to reclaim the customs and traditions of the past and repair the bonds that had sustained them since the days of slavery.

The annual church basket dinners and family reunions that had once served as cultural and social get-togethers no longer fulfilled their greater needs. Negro History Week, which had been established in 1926 by historian Carter Woodson, had expanded into Black History Month. This provided an annual opportunity for communities to celebrate the history and the advancement of their race and share them with the rest of society. Once the birthday of Martin Luther King, Jr., became a national holiday, celebrating King's life provided communities with another chance to form connections. Black school reunions—generally occurring every one to three years— have also become popular as a means of bringing communities back together. Fielding Draffen of Kansas City founded

"The Missouri Negro High School Reunion Committee," an association of the state's black high schools, in 1990. The reunions are held on Labor Day weekends in various locations.

The traditional Emancipation Day, long celebrated in Missouri on August 4, continues to be an occasion for large gatherings of African Americans. The celebration on this date, which began even before emancipation, is of uncertain origin. One theory holds that since slaveholders celebrated Independence Day on July 4, some owners provided a slave holiday the following month. Another says that free blacks celebrated August 4 as Black Independence Day and as a day of protest because it was on August 1, 1834, that England had freed the slaves in the West Indies. In any case, a celebration at Clinton, Missouri, began in 1892 or before and continues to draw a large following today.

Juneteenth celebrations also became popular in Missouri as African Americans continued to reassemble the vestiges of their customs and traditions. This celebration originated in Texas. Although President Abraham Lincoln issued the Emancipation Proclamation on January 1, 1863, freeing those slaves held in the Confederate states, Texas slaves were not aware of their emancipation until June 19, 1865, when Major General Gordon Granger publicly read a special order from President Lincoln in Galveston, Texas. The day was chosen for celebration as early as 1866, and the name shortened to Juneteenth. Missouri communities began to celebrate this holiday during the 1970s.

The seven-day cultural holiday known as Kwanzaa, December 26 through January 1, is now widely celebrated in Missouri. Maulana Karenga initiated this holiday at California State University in Long Beach in the mid-1960s. Kwanzaa is a time in which families bond and reaffirm their ties to their past and to the community. Central to Kwanzaa is "nguzo saba," seven principles that combine African American values and African tradition.

The celebration begins with an opening ceremony, and each day is devoted to one of the seven principles: unity, self-determination, collective work and responsibility, cooperative economics, purpose, creativity, and faith. A special candelabra, called the "kinara," is placed in the center of a table. A black candle, representing race and unity, is placed in the center of the candelabra and is lit on the first day. Three green candles, representing home and the continent of Africa, are placed on the left side, and three red candles, representing blood, the liquid of life, are placed on the right.

On the second day, the black candle and one of the green candles are lit. Alternating from left to right, a new candle is lit for each day, and the previous days' candles are relit, until all are lit on the seventh day. The feast of Kwanzaa is called the "Karamu," and the place where it is held is usually decorated with red, black, and green.

Although occasions such as Kwanzaa and Juneteenth are relatively new celebrations for Missourians, the traditional foods, music, and storytelling are still the principle means of observing these holidays. Food continues to be the centerpiece of the celebrations. Missouri's African American cooks keep to the tradition of simple cooking seasoned to perfection that has been passed down through the generations, and soul food is still served for special meals.

Lillie Mabel Hall of St. Louis, who served as a master in the Missouri Cultural Heritage Center's master/apprentice program in 1988, helps keep the tradition alive. She learned to cook from her mother and grandmother. Hall, the first African American to be admitted to St. Louis University, claims expertise in such traditional foods as chicken-foot stew and wild greens, as well as fish and wild game cookery. The Missouri Folk Arts Program at the University of Missouri provides a means of preserving such cultural traditions and enables skilled artisans and practitioners to pass their skills on.

Traditions are often passed along through stories. The oral tradition of storytelling remains a time-honored means of sharing the African American experience. From the villages and kingdoms of Africa, slaves had brought with them their oral traditions. In the fields where they labored and the cabins where they prayed and slept, they refined that tradition; it found honor in the community and a place in the hearts of generations of African Americans. One of the brightest voices in Missouri is that of master storyteller Gladys Coggswell of Frankford, who has made it her life's work to maintain the African American oral tradition in the state. She earned the title of master folk artist in the area of storytelling through the Missouri traditional artist and apprenticeship program at the University of Missouri–Columbia.

Coggswell has collected oral histories and narratives across the state, and her extensive repertoire includes stories about heroic individuals, the adventures of ghosts and talking animals, and family tales. She travels and performs extensively, and she is also a popular workshop leader, teacher, and lecturer. As the founder of the "By Word of Mouth" Storytelling Guild, she sponsors an annual storytelling festival and retreat.

Traditional forms are passed on, and refined, by new generations. Writers like St. Louisans Gerald Early, Maya Angelou, Ntozake Shange, and Patricia McKissack have become nationally known tellers of both old and new tales. Their stories are sometimes inspired by the tales of old, and sometimes by the experiences captured so well in black music; the blues, jazz, ragtime, gospel, and Negro spirituals continue to swell the hearts and spirits of African Americans.

Within the movement to reclaim and preserve the early history and institutions of African American communities, schools have played a crucial role. Lincoln University, which now draws students of all races and ages, still stands as a beacon of light to those who want to learn about their past and forge a better future. As Antonio Holland demonstrates in *The*

Dr. Arvarh Strickland, MU's first black professor, has introduced countless students to African American history since he came to the university in 1969. (MU Publications and Alumni Communication)

Dream Continued: A Pictorial History, published in 1991 for the 125th anniversary of the university's founding, the school has truly become a dream fulfilled. The soldiers of the Sixty-second and Sixty-fifth U.S. Colored Infantries who pooled their meager resources to build an institution of learning have left a lasting legacy. The university's new Inman Page Library Archive holds a major collection of documents and photographs relating to the African American experience in Missouri collected by the late Lorenzo Greene and other scholars.

The University of Missouri–Columbia has established the Arvarh E. Strickland Distinguished Professorship, a million-dollar endowed chair, to recognize the contributions of the first African American professor at the university. Strickland, professor emeritus of history, came to Columbia in 1969, and has since served the university in many capacities. The university began offering undergraduate and graduate courses in African American history in 1969, and the next year it established a black studies program, with Strickland as its first director. Hundreds of men and women, both black and white, have been introduced to African American life and culture at the university.

An organization seeking to reclaim and preserve examples of that culture for future generations is the Black Archives of Mid-America. Founded by Horace Peterson III in 1974, the archive is the largest depository of African American memorabilia, artifacts, and documented history in the Midwest. The archive is located in the renovated historic Vine Street District in Kansas City, which is noted for its jazz history. Kansas City is also home to the Negro Leagues Baseball Museum, and the city's jazz legacy has been preserved by the 18th and Vine Historic Jazz District project.

Also in Kansas City, the American Royal, one of the oldest and most important horse shows in America, honors Tom Bass, who put on a horse show to raise funds for the Kansas City Fire Department in 1892. The "Tom Bass Riders," a group of black riders carrying the name of the first "horse whisperer" are a popular feature of the show.

Likewise, St. Louis honors black citizens and groups who have made important contributions to culture. The Scott Joplin House is now a state historic site in St. Louis. Joplin and his second wife, Belle Hayden Joplin, lived in the four-family dwelling from 1901 until 1903. The house was designated a national historic landmark in 1976 and saved from demolition by a neighborhood development corporation. The home was donated to the state for restoration in 1983 and opened to the public in October 1991.

The St. Louis Black Repertory Company, founded in 1976, presents a full season of theater, dance, and other creative experiences from September through June to heighten the cultural awareness of the African American experience at its new theater. In honor of its famous black citizens, St. Louisans have also created the St. Louis Walk of Fame by designating a section of University City sidewalk for the placement of bronze stars and plaques in tribute to such notable African Americans as Josephine Baker, Katherine Dunham, Chuck Berry, and Tina Turner, to name a few. Each year, two new names are added to the list. This project began in 1988.

The state capitol in Jefferson City displays busts of notable Missourians, including Josephine Baker and Tom Bass, as well as many photographs and artifacts relating to African American life in the state. In recent years the Missouri Department of Natural Resources has developed a number of exhibits celebrating African American life in Missouri and is now developing a civil rights museum.

Outside the major cities of Missouri, groups recognize the local people and places that were important in African American history. The George Washington Carver National Monument and nature trail in Diamond pays tribute to the noted black scientist. In the late 1980s, the Concerned Citizens of Boonville decided to purchase the black Sumner School building and turn it into a community center. Some alumni of Sedalia's Hubbard School purchased that facility, and under the leadership of the Lincoln-Hubbard Alumni Association of Sedalia are preserving and restoring the building. Columbia and Warrensburg hold Blind Boone festivals each year to celebrate the life of Missouri's ragtime pioneer.

The tiny towns of Canton, in Lewis County, and Arrow Rock, in Saline County, have also undertaken restoration projects. The Lincoln School Restoration Project of Canton is restoring the redbrick, one-room Lincoln School that began serving black citizens in 1880. The Friends of Arrow Rock have restored Brown's Chapel Freewill Baptist Church, which was built in 1871, and are restoring the Negro Masonic Hall.

Descendants of its founding members are also restoring the Freewill Baptist Church in Pennytown.

As African Americans continue to move into Missouri's mainstream they are also moving to guard and protect the treasures of their past—their customs and traditions—and carry this heritage with them on their journey. The tradition of entrepreneurship was nearly destroyed by the demolition squads of urban renewal. Many black owners of the small businesses that were shoveled into the dustbins by the land clearance programs came to view the process as "urban removal." Since most black businesses were located near black neighborhoods, the efforts to clear away substandard housing caught them in its path. The wheels of progress ground the businesses into the dust. Though many of the poorly planned and badly managed housing projects, such as Pruitt-Igoe, were pulled down in the 1970s, the black businesses that had been there before were gone forever.

Black-owned businesses also suffered when they were abandoned by those they served. The passing of the Public Accommodations Act made it possible for African Americans to eat and sleep where they pleased, attend theaters, and patronize other service establishments. The black public, which was the mainstay of most black businesses, took the opportunity to spend their money elsewhere. Most black businesses were unable to get financing to relocate to established business districts. Lending institutions were not eager to invest money in what they viewed as fledgling enterprises.

But the spirit of black entrepreneurship had survived decades of hard times and tight money. Though wavering on wobbly legs, black barber and beauty establishments, restaurants, and janitorial and maid services held on and established economic footholds. Some entrepreneurs expanded their areas of expertise; they seized new opportunities, and for many, their daring and dedication paid off.

Old housing, new housing in Columbia. (State Historical Society of Missouri, Columbia; photo of new apartments by A. E. Schroeder)

The Black Pages, telephone directories in Kansas City and St. Louis, tell the story of entrepreneurship: page after page lists the number and variety of African American businesses available in these cities. Early in the 1980s, African Americans formed the Black Chamber of Commerce of Kansas City, and enterprising black businesspeople can be found in most small towns and cities in Missouri.

One such enterprising individual is Inez Yeargan Kaiser. To Kaiser, "Whatever the mind believes and conceives, it can achieve," is more than just a motto. These words have set the pace for many of her lifetime achievements. A Kansas City author, businesswoman, and mass media specialist, Kaiser grew up in Kansas City, Kansas, received a master's degree in home economics from Columbia University in New York in 1958, and went on to train in market research and marketing at Rockhurst College in Kansas City. She taught elementary and high school and worked in civil service before founding her own business, Inez Kaiser and Associates, which specializes in public relations, advertising, market research, and technical assistance, with offices in Kansas City and Washington, D. C. Her clientele has included many major corporations throughout the country.

Her syndicated columns have appeared in many black newspapers, and she is the author of several books, including *Inez Kaiser's Original Soul Food Cookbook.* She has appeared on national television as well as local radio and television shows. Her many honors and awards include the Golden Mike Award, presented by American Women in Radio and Television, and the Ertha M. White Award for the Most Outstanding Black Businesswoman in the country. An active member of the Episcopal church, Kaiser is a well-known community worker who serves on numerous boards. She is one of Kansas City's most distinguished citizens.

It is clear that the spirit that fired the dreams of the freed-

men and women in the early years is still alive and well in
Missouri. The traditions of self-help and mutual aid also continue in African American communities. The NAACP main-
tains chapters in many cities and towns, monitoring civil
rights for African Americans. The Urban League, having been
in the employment business since 1918, still offers assistance
to African Americans in search of jobs.

Annie Malone's Children and Family Service Center of St.
Louis, formerly the St. Louis Colored Orphans Home, founded in 1878 by members of the Colored Women's Temperance
Union, carries on its mission of service to single-parent families and operates a twenty-four–hour family crisis center.
Annie Pope Turnbo-Malone donated money and land for con-
struction of its current building, which was completed in
1922, and the home was renamed in her honor in 1946. The
Black Economic Union of Greater Kansas City is a community development corporation, which devotes itself to the economic, social, and physical revitalization of blighted neighborhoods and develops entrepreneurs and small businesses.

Sororities, fraternities, clubs, and neighborhood associa-
tions throughout the state provide a variety of services to
African Americans. They contribute scholarships, assist families in crisis and help maintain the quality of African American
life. Black communities, broken up by the impact of progress,
have picked themselves up once more, dusted themselves off,
and are putting the pieces back together again.

Each time they have been forced to reconstruct, they have
also rediscovered, or sometimes reinvented, their cultural identities. Long before Debbye Turner, a University of Missouri–
Columbia student, was named Miss America in 1990, African
Americans had come to grips with the concept that black
could also be beautiful. The black power movement of the
1960s swept the country and radically changed the way most
African Americans viewed themselves. They stopped trying to
straighten their hair and trimmed and shaped it into what

Miss Missouri Debbye Turner in 1989. Turner went on to win the Miss America competition. (*Columbia Daily Tribune,* photo by David Pulliam)

became known as the Afro. They no longer hid their hair under scarves and kerchiefs but began to use those accessories as items of adornment. They began to reclaim the decorative hairstyles of their African ancestors and to add a few touches of their own. They braided, beaded, and wrapped their hair into attractive styles and pierced their noses as well as their ears.

Captured by a new sense of identity, some changed their names and the clothes they wore, reflecting in both their African heritage. "Dashikas," African-styled shirts, became popular. No longer ashamed of their past, blacks began to identify with their ancestry. By the time Missourians were celebrating a black Miss America, the black community had come to identify itself as African American. The practice of

African traditions such as wearing kente cloth or jumping over a broom at weddings had become commonplace. Their children had become Kenya, Ashanta, and Mali, identifying their kinship with the Dark Continent.

Like their ancestors, many African Americans today still refer to one another as "brother" and "sister," even if they are unrelated. "Aunts" and "uncles" are sometimes just friends and neighbors who claim "fictive kinship" or membership in an extended family. When African Americans pass one another on the streets and highways, they are likely to acknowledge one another's presence, even though they are strangers.

When they travel throughout the state, African Americans tend to keep a sharp eye out for restaurants where they might enjoy the food of their history. Collard greens, cornbread, yams, and beans are welcome delights and familiar sights at the table. As in the time of slavery, Saturday night is often the time when African Americans pursue their own amusements. It may be going to a church fish fry, swaying to soul music, or just getting together with neighbors.

Spiritual worship services and mournful burials testify to a deeply rooted oral tradition. The music which pours from their souls bears witness to the emotional connection that ties them to their past. In developing their own customs and traditions, African Americans have simply adapted their cultural heritage and folkways to effectively serve them through the long, often painful experiences they have endured in their struggle to make Missouri their home.

FOR MORE READING

Blind Boone: Missouri's Ragtime Pioneer, by Jack A. Batterson (Columbia: University of Missouri Press, 1998), gives a detailed account of J. W. "Blind" Boone's life and career within the context of the cultural and musical environment of his time. Born to a black mother and a white Union soldier during the chaos of the Civil War, Boone brought his music to white audiences and music of the European tradition to black audiences in concerts throughout the United States and Canada.

The Colored Aristocracy of St. Louis, by Cyprian Clamorgan, edited by Julie Winch (Columbia: University of Missouri Press, 1999), is one of the very few works that deals with black elite life in the years prior to the Civil War. The introduction and notes by Winch provide vital information about St. Louis and its free black families in the mid-nineteenth century.

Dancing to a Black Man's Tune: A Life of Scott Joplin, by Susan Curtis (Columbia: University of Missouri Press, 1994), an interpretative biography of the "King of Ragtime," examines Joplin's life as it related to the life of the various communities in which he lived and worked and assesses his legacy. The book includes many photographs.

Discovering African American St. Louis: A Guide to Historic Sites, by John A. Wright (St. Louis: Missouri Historical Society Press, 1994), revised 2002, contains everything you want to know and every place you want to see relating to African American historical sites in St. Louis.

Four Hundred Years without a Comb, by Willie Morrow (San Diego: Black Publishers of San Diego, Morrow's Unlimited, 1973) provides a historical perspective on black hair and its care in the New World.

James Milton Turner and the Promise of America, by Gary R. Kremer (Columbia: University of Missouri Press, 1991), is a wonderful biography of the ex-slave who became a fierce civil rights advocate in Missouri and who was instrumental in establishing schools for blacks following the Civil War.

The Kansas City Monarchs: Champions of Black Baseball, by Janet Bruce (Lawrence: University Press of Kansas, 1985), is based on interviews with players and others who remember the vibrant community life in black Kansas City and what the Monarchs meant to it. The text is enhanced with more than ninety photographs.

Missouri's Black Heritage, revised edition by Lorenzo J. Greene, Gary R. Kremer, and Antonio F. Holland (Columbia: University of Missouri Press, 1993). Originally published in 1980, this compelling book provides a breathtaking account of the rich history of African Americans in Missouri. It is a rare treasure, drawing on many documentary resources to explore the history of African Americans in Missouri.

Not So Simple: The "Simple" Stories by Langston Hughes, by Donna Akiba Sullivan Harper (Columbia: University of Missouri Press, 1996), takes a scholarly look at the satirical stories by Langston Hughes that feature the character Jessie B. Semple and provides new insights into both the famous author and his characters.

Working with Carter G. Woodson, the Father of Black History, edited by Arvarh E. Strickland (Baton Rouge: Louisiana State University Press, 1989), is the diary of Lorenzo J. Greene, written during the years 1928 to 1930, when he served as a research assistant to the driving force behind the Association for the Study of Negro Life and History. It offers a richly detailed, behind-the-scenes look at this ambitious undertaking.

INDEX

Page numbers in boldface refer to photos.

ABOUT THE AUTHOR

Rose M. Nolen is a columnist for the *Columbia Missourian*.